"The strength of Schlegelmilch's v
autism-professional voice—one that is no-nonsense, down-to-earth, and clear as a bell. Mix that in with his deep understanding of ASD and the whole teenage 'thing,' seasoned with wry asides and warmed with compassion, and you have a highly useful, compelling, and unusual book."

—*Susan Senator, blogger, parent, and author of*
The Autism Mom's Survival Guide

"Andrew Schlegelmilch's new book, *Parenting ASD Teens*, is a clear, detailed, and much-needed look at the parenting of teens on the spectrum. His years of experience with ASD teens and their parents at Orion Academy come through in the realistic information and the thoughtful, professional discussion. This is a must-read book for both parents and clinicians living and working with this population."

—*Kathryn Stewart, PhD, Executive Director and Founder*
of Orion Academy and author of Helping a Child with
Nonverbal Learning Disorder or Asperger's Disorder

"While the title of Dr. Schlegelmilch's book is *Parenting ASD Teens*, this volume is a wealth of information and advice useful to any parent or professional who works with teens or adults. He is extremely knowledgeable and obviously cares for these kids. I would recommend the book as a preparation for parents for the many challenges and changes that life will bring. It covers a breadth of topics, both outside and inside of the classroom. This is stuff we as parents and professionals need to know!"

—*Luby Aczel, parent of a son with Asperger Syndrome*
and Executive Director of The Specialists Guild

"Educational, insightful, and encouraging. In *Parenting ASD Teens*, Dr. Schlegelmilch gives valuable information regarding the challenges facing adolescent ASD teens and young adults. Dr. Schlegelmilch offers practical advice about how ASD teens learn and grow towards independence. I would strongly recommend this book to parents."

—*Karra M. Barber, author of* The Social and Life Skills MeNu

PARENTING ASD TEENS

of related interest

Parenting a Teen or Young Adult with Asperger Syndrome (Autism Spectrum Disorder)
325 Ideas, Insights, Tips and Strategies
Brenda Boyd
ISBN 978 1 84905 282 5
eISBN 978 0 85700 587 8

The Social and Life Skills MeNu
A Skill Building Workbook for Adolescents with Autism Spectrum Disorders
Karra M. Barber
ISBN 978 1 84905 861 2
eISBN 978 0 85700 433 8

60 Social Situations and Discussion Starters to Help Teens on the Autism Spectrum Deal with Friendships, Feelings, Conflict and More
Seeing the Big Picture
Lisa A. Timms
ISBN 978 1 84905 862 9
eISBN 978 0 85700 468 0

Making Sense of Sex
A Forthright Guide to Puberty, Sex and Relationships for People with Asperger's Syndrome
Sarah Attwood
Illustrated by Jonathon Powell
ISBN 978 1 84310 374 5
eISBN 978 1 84642 797 8

Life After High School
A Guide for Students with Disabilities and Their Families
Susan Yellin and Christina Cacioppo Bertsch
ISBN 978 1 84905 828 5
eISBN 978 0 85700 302 7

The Wonderful World of Work
A Workbook for Asperteens
Jeanette Purkis
ISBN 978 1 84905 499 7
eISBN 978 0 85700 923 4

PARENTING ASD TEENS

A GUIDE TO MAKING IT UP AS YOU GO

ANDREW SCHLEGELMILCH

Jessica Kingsley *Publishers*
London and Philadelphia

First published in 2014
by Jessica Kingsley Publishers
73 Collier Street
London N1 9BE, UK
and
400 Market Street, Suite 400
Philadelphia, PA 19106, USA

www.jkp.com

Library of Congress Cataloging in Publication Data
Schlegelmilch, Andrew.
Parenting ASD teens : a guide to making it up as you go / Andrew Schlegelmilch.
pages cm
Includes bibliographical references and index.
ISBN 978-1-84905-975-6 (alk. paper)
1. Parenting. 2. Parents of autistic children. 3. Children
with autism spectrum disorders. 4. Teenagers
with disabilities. 5. Teenager and parent. I. Title.
HQ773.8.S35 2014
649'.15--dc23
2013048196

British Library Cataloguing in Publication Data
A CIP catalogue record for this book is available from the British Library

ISBN 978 1 84905 975 6
eISBN 978 0 85700 921 0

Printed and bound in Great Britain

This book is dedicated to Devon

ACKNOWLEDGMENTS

Writing this book would not have been possible without the experience and support of the students, parents, administration, and my colleagues at Orion Academy in Moraga, California. My first day on the job in August 2007 felt like going to work on another planet. Now it feels like home.

This book would also not have been possible without help from Nick M., who gave his time and expertise selflessly and without hesitation.

CONTENTS

PREFACE

My work with ASD individuals and their families over the years has taught me two things about what it takes to be a successful parent to an ASD teen. First, the more of an expertise parents build in areas such as education, neurology, psychology, relationships, and independent living, the more confident they feel in their parenting. Second, the more time they spend assembling a competent team of professionals and other supportive adults to help them in their parenting, the better they sleep.

This book is the summary of much of my work in private practice and academic settings with individuals on the Spectrum and their families. It is my intention to give the parent insight into the experience of their child and the places where they live and learn in order to help the parent be as effective as they can be. Thank you for letting me be a part of your team.

PART I

GETTING TO KNOW YOUR TEEN

CHAPTER 1

WHAT ARE AUTISM SPECTRUM DISORDERS?

I remember very distinctly my first interaction with a Spectrum teen. I saw this boy sitting by himself and looking despondent, so I decided to see if I could help. Sitting down beside the boy I asked him if anything was wrong. After a pause of a second or two, I was surprised when he shared that he had just completed the first few classes of the first day of school and he could tell that this was going to be a hard year. He was unsure if he would make it through the year, especially considering he had just barely passed all of his classes the previous year. I was surprised at the succinct and insightful assessment of his current state since my training stated that people on the Spectrum had communication and socialization problems. I mentioned to him that the doubt he was feeling was common and he was likely dealing with some "first day jitters." I sat in silence, waiting for him to take his turn to speak. At this point, teens usually say something about how their situation is special, or there is no way I could understand their experience, or thanks for the great advice, or that they still feel anxious or despondent, or something like that. This student gave me nothing. In fact, he had not moved a muscle the whole time we were talking. He had not even looked at me to confirm who was speaking to him (I was new at the school and this was our first interaction). Unable to wait any more, I repeated some comforting and encouraging phrases to him about first days being tough and he cut me off and said sternly, "You already said that to me. If you can't come up with anything new to say then you must really suck at your job!"

Raising children on the Spectrum requires advanced parenting skills, and full commitment. No one I have met has been half-way successful in parenting a child on the Spectrum. Parents seem to be "all in," or completely disengaged. It is no surprise that many of the experts that give you advice on raising your Autism Spectrum Disorder (ASD) child are actually parents of children on the Spectrum. I think the reason for this is that successfully raising a child on the Spectrum is such an enormous task and huge endeavor that many parents see it as a waste if they do not share their experience and knowledge with other parents. I have met parents that have become amateur experts in Sensory Integration, classroom management, Individual Education Plans (IEPs) and their associated laws, behavior modification, neurology and neuropsychology, nutrition, job training, and all sorts of areas where they felt their child was getting insufficient care, or just wanted to better understand the experience of their child.

I call these parents Native Experts, and it is for these parents, and parents who aspire to be like Native Experts, that I write this book. Because of the growing amount of quality information we have on ASDs, and the high level of interest there appears to be regarding it, it is my intention for this book to be as much of a discussion as it will be a description of best practices in parenting ASD individuals. I want the reader's experience with this book to be dynamic. Rather than looking for ways that this book does not apply to your specific situation (an activity my ASD students and clients seem to spend a huge amount of time doing), I want the reader to look for direction and ideas for making their parenting journey not only more tolerable, but exciting and fulfilling.

To that end, it is important that we are all on the same page regarding terminology. If you continue further in your own research you will find that there are disagreements on and confusion about terminology surrounding the ASD diagnoses. As I write this manuscript, there is a growing debate on whether or not the Autism community is still well-served by the current labeling and diagnostic system given the high level of individual differences within the ASD community. Creating and agreeing upon a common language to describe what we are working with is important in science because much of science is collaborative. I absolutely prefer a collaborative approach in the work I do, and especially with parents, so below is a list of some of the names and labels I will be using throughout the book.

The Spectrum or the Category

There are at least two ways professionals are classifying Autism. One is using a Continuous System, and the other is using a Categorical System. The Autism Spectrum actually refers to the former, a Continuous System of classification. Professionals can assess an individual on a number of different skills or continua (more than one continuum) to create a diagnostic profile of an individual. If you think about a line drawn horizontally on a page connecting two dots, this is a graphic depiction of a continuum. When professionals use the term "Autism Spectrum" they are usually referring to continua of "functionality," and, more specifically, functionality in areas such as life skills, communication skills, social skills, and academic skills. When a professional looks at a number of different continua together in one report, this is often referred to as a "profile."

Professionals try to use terms like Autism, Asperger Syndrome, Non-verbal Learning Disability (or Disorder), and others in a methodical way. These terms actually refer to the Categorical System of classification. Professionals compare what they are observing in an individual to lists of symptoms so they know what label (i.e., diagnosis) to assign to the person they are seeing. Diagnoses are important for several reasons. Most importantly, they give people a common language that provides specific and efficient communication of an idea. This is a huge help if more than one person needs to treat an individual. Also, diagnosis directs treatment. It gives the professional a place to start treatment, and it gives the consumer the ability to evaluate the quality of treatment.

Both systems have their upsides and their downsides, which is why professionals often use both systems in both assessment and treatment. The Continuous System allows for intense specificity (individualization of treatment), but the assessment process can become cumbersome. It is also difficult to communicate with others what you are seeing (i.e., assessment) and how you are responding (i.e., treatment). The Categorical System is much better for communication, but also much more clunky and less specific. In treatment, I usually prefer to start out with the Categorical System (e.g., assign someone a label that others will understand) and then use the Continuous System for ongoing intervention and assessment.

The Common Variables and the Overlap

The Autism Spectrum actually refers to a set of qualities, skills, and abilities all individuals have that professionals can assess for strengths and weaknesses, assets and deficits, or absence or presence to a greater or lesser degree. To make a diagnosis in the Autism Spectrum Disorders, professionals look primarily at Social Functioning, Executive Functioning, and Sensory Integration. For the most part, the variables of interest in the Autism Spectrum manifest largely at the level of the brain. Autism and related disorders are neurological disorders, and much of the symptomatology is only observable under certain circumstances and if you know what to look for. For instance, a person's ability in reading comprehension (an activity that can span all three areas listed above) cannot really be assessed unless they were given a task specifically for that purpose, and someone knew how to interpret their observations in a meaningful and useful way.

It should be noted that there are broad patterns of functionality and dysfunction among individuals on the Spectrum. For instance, most people on the Spectrum have some difficulty in developing and mastering social skills, but this ability can vary from person to person, even when people have the same diagnosis. Big-picture thinking (e.g., inferring underlying meaning by listening to discussion comments) is also a challenge for most people on the Spectrum, but again, functioning varies between individuals. Everyone (ASD individuals or so-called Neurotypicals [NTs]) seems to learn social skills and big-picture thinking through practice, but most people on the Spectrum seem to struggle with one or more parts of that process of learning.

It is because of this seeming overlap of symptoms between people diagnosed with Autism and those diagnosed with another disorder called Asperger Syndrome (AS) that many professionals believe Autism and AS are different expressions of the same disorder. I have heard some clients suggest that they have "Autism-light" (referring to an AS diagnosis). Other professionals believe that diagnoses of Autism and AS are categorically different from one another. They generally acknowledge the symptom overlap, but maintain that the diagnoses belong in discrete categories. Admittedly, in most cases, these two ideologies can easily co-exist. I will do my best in this book to appeal to both schools of thought, and identify when I am siding with one or the other.

Social Skills

Humans are social animals. I do not believe that ASD individuals are unable to acquire adequate social skills or are unable to improve their Social Functioning. What I have found is that the way in which NTs learn social skills is not an easy or natural process for ASD individuals. People learn most social skills from their peers, and the process of learning social skills happens through the accumulated peer experiences we have over a lifetime, but especially in childhood. I often tell my clients and students that teens really do not learn social skills from adults very well, and certainly not from professionals (other than, of course, how to interact with those adults and professionals).

Most people actually learn the vast majority of their social skills from their peers in dynamic, reciprocal, social interactions. A typical interaction can start with Child A looking sideways at Child B. Based on the context (physical environment, the children's relationship to one another, what happened right before the sideways glance, etc.), Child B will respond in a noticeable way. Child A will incorporate this response into his next behavior (e.g., laughing or nudging someone else), and back and forth this interaction will go, each individual making slight adjustments to their response based on the feedback they are getting from their social interaction partner and the general environment. Hundreds of adjustments can be made in each interaction in super-dynamic social situations, each adjustment based on assumptions and hypotheses tested and confirmed. Imagine all the data one can gather about socializing in a single day.

What if you struggle with interpreting the responses from others? What if your interpretation of the responses of others is perpetually incorrect or you find the information fundamentally indecipherable? This is what happens for most ASD individuals I see. On various levels, individuals on the Spectrum struggle with reciprocal social interactions. They report to me that the intentions and behaviors of others are often a mystery. To me, a native English speaker, it would be like taking an Economics class in French. I know a few French words, but not nearly enough to follow a lecture, read the text, or participate in a group project. I would fall further and further behind in the class and probably give up because no one is teaching me French (it's an Economics class, after all).

Consequently, this is why professionals are recommending early intervention, and why children with early identification and intervention fare so much better than those with later or no intervention. If you teach children some of the basics of socializing early, help the student calibrate their interpretation of social interactions and their responses, put them in an environment where this process can happen as much as possible with a professional who can help guide the progress and correct mistakes, then social skills will develop.

Deficits in Social Functioning have a profound impact on daily living. Individuals use social skills to interact with peers, teachers, principals, physicians, policemen, parents, and all the other people who are necessary for us to learn how to navigate through life and be safe. As an adult, one needs to be able to interact appropriately with a variety of people in different roles and in society such as bosses, romantic partners, aging parents, and work subordinates. People get different treatment based on their ability to master social situations and the rules associated with those situations. Good social skills are essential for success in nearly every aspect of living.

Executive Functioning

Executive Functioning (EF) is an enormous term that means something a little different to everyone you ask. In the case of ASDs, EF is a term used to describe the skills related to planning, organizing, prioritizing, categorizing, predicting, and strategizing, among other things. For instance, EF is one of the primary mental departments that is used when a student is assigned homework. When it comes to homework, for instance, EF skills are associated with:

- attention, including ignoring and focusing on various stimuli
- looking in the correct place (e.g., written on the board, on the syllabus, listening to the teacher at the end of class) to find the homework assignment
- copying it down in a place you will look or be able to find it when you get home
- bringing home the appropriate materials to do the homework
- setting aside enough time to do the work
- pacing yourself and taking breaks during the homework process
- deciding how much time to spend on each assignment
- prioritizing the assignments
- completing the homework fully (and remembering to read the directions)
- checking your work
- knowing when to stop working on an assignment
- remembering to take work back to school
- turning in the completed homework
- about 100 other tasks along the way.

When the general public sees a person with an EF deficit, they often conclude that the person is lazy, disorganized, undermotivated, or negligent. What they fail to realize is that activities such as completing a homework assignment represent multistep and complex brain activities. Items such as day-planners or smartphones can be a very helpful stand-in for some steps in the process (such as setting an alarm on your phone to remind you to start doing homework), but there are a number of places where people with EF deficits can get tripped up along the way. Remediating and accounting for EF deficits can take a considerable amount of time, practice, and thoughtful energy, but remediation is possible, and most people who work at it experience considerable success.

Sensory Integration

It seems to me that it is possible that each individual has a unique sensory experience (e.g., do you see the color red the way I do?), but based on the stories I hear from ASD individuals and what I have observed, people on the Spectrum seem to have a sensory experience that ranges from slightly different to completely different from the average NT.

First, ASD individuals are often noticeably dominant in one sensory modality over the others. It is true that most people can identify a sensory dominance (e.g., I am equally dominant in visual and tactile but have a very limited sense of taste), but the sensory dominance of the ASD individual seems to be a major factor in how they interact with the world in terms of learning, experiencing, socializing, and general living. I hear over and over that information presented in the non-dominant modality (e.g., writing something on the board [that they have to perceive visually] when the person is auditorily dominant) means the person does not encode (i.e., store for future use) the information at all. Either there is no memory of the stimulus or the memory cannot be recalled. There seems to be no end of frustration on the part of the ASD individual, the parent, the teacher, or other interested parties when communication breaks down due to a sensory issue. Interestingly, sensory dominance is one factor a professional can examine to help effectively assess and treat an ASD individual.

Second, ASD individuals seem to struggle with filtering sensory information. Most people's brains do the sensory filtering naturally and effortlessly. Our brains can also be trained to respond to certain sensory information (e.g., someone saying your name) while filtering out other information (e.g., a room full of conversations). From what I can tell, many ASD individuals have no such filter, or have an inefficient filter. For this reason and others, sensory overload is a much more common experience for individuals on the Spectrum, and managing sensory input can be a taxing and exhausting chore for the ASD individual. Whereas the average NT individual does not really give much thought day-to-day on managing the sensory environment, most ASD individuals think about it and consciously adjust to their sensory needs on a regular basis.

Finally, our brains create a narrative about the world and what is happening around us partly through a process called Sensory Integration. Our memories of our last holiday meal with the family are not just a series of still images of our family that we can recall, or a recollection of the different conversation topics. We remember how the meal we shared tasted and smelled, we remember the conversation we had around the dinner table, and the relative brightness of the room. Our brains weave together information from all active senses to create the memory of that meal. ASD individuals, on the other hand, report that their sensory experience can be limited to just one source at a time, and especially when the environment is rich in sensory input (like a chaotic family gathering). This can be because the overall level of input is overly intense and some senses effectively "shut off" to control the flow of information, or a sensory modality (often smell or touch) is overly sensitive and drowns out all the other information. ASD individuals often report sensory overload where they have the experience of "rebooting," or the higher brain functions essentially shutting down for a while as they regain their faculties. This looks much like the "freeze" response in the fight, flight, or freeze method of responding to anxiety or danger.

As you can see, it is challenging to describe each of these three areas of deficit or challenge in a way that is separate and discrete from the other two. Most situations people encounter will require skill use in all of these areas. For instance, going to the mall to shop involves interacting with store clerks (social), planning your route (EF), and dealing with crowds (sensory). Even though there are some subtle and not-so-subtle differences between people on the Spectrum with different diagnoses, in nearly all cases there will be some shared difficulty in each of these three areas.

The Major Categories

Asperger Syndrome

Several years ago very few people had heard of Asperger Syndrome (AS; also referred to as Asperger Disorder), and even fewer could define it. Times have changed, though. Below are some of the formal features professionals look for in order to diagnose AS:

- Impairment in social interaction:
  - problems with non-verbal communication (e.g., poor eye contact)
  - problems making friends with same-age peers
  - lack of social or emotional reciprocity (i.e., the give-and-take in relationships).

- Restricted, repetitive, or stereotyped behaviors:
  - intense preoccupations (e.g., everything is about dinosaurs)
  - rigid, inflexible, or ritualistic routines
  - repetitive motor mannerisms (e.g., hand-flapping)
  - preoccupation with parts of an object (e.g., spinning a wheel instead of playing with the Matchbox car).

- Symptoms witnessed above cause impairment.

- No language delay (see Autism definition later in this chapter for comparison).

- No significant cognitive delay (these children have at least average IQ).

- Symptoms are not better described as another disorder.

These are based on the *DSM-IV* criteria (American Psychiatric Association [APA] 1994). It should be noted that the newest version of the *Diagnostic and Statistical Manual* (*DSM-5*; APA 2013) does not include a specific diagnosis of AS, but instead combines many Autism-like disorders into one diagnostic category. Many parents and professionals continue to find it useful to distinguish between AS and other ASDs.

AS was included in a class of disorders called Pervasive Developmental Disorders (PDD) in the *DSM-IV*. In that list is Autism and Pervasive Developmental Disorder—Not Otherwise Specified (PDD-NOS), both of which I will mention later. Now, many people are diagnosed with AS as children around the age of 4 or 5. The reason for children being diagnosed at this age is that this is the age when children start doing things where they have to socialize with their peers. Preschool and kindergarten usually begin for most children around this time, and children start to get observed by professional adults (e.g., teachers) and have their behavior systematically compared to other children, and questions start to arise.

More and more, however, I am meeting people and working with people who have had a "late diagnosis." I would say any diagnosis after the start of high school can be considered a late diagnosis when considering PDD. Some of these people find the diagnosis a relief; some find it devastating. Research is fairly consistent in telling us that early diagnosis and intervention leads to the best results, but nearly everyone who sets out to improve their lives, regardless of their age, succeeds in some way.

Autism

This was referred to as Autistic Disorder in the *DSM-IV*, and Autism Spectrum Disorders in the *DSM-5* (2013). Here is the *DSM-5* definition:

- Impairment in social interaction and communication.

- Restricted, repetitive, or stereotyped behaviors.

- Delays or impairments occur early in development.

- Disturbances cause significant impairment.

It is possible that comparing the *DSM-IV* Asperger definition with the *DSM-5* Autism Spectrum Disorders definition can create some confusion. There are a couple of things parents should consider when differentiating between an Autism diagnosis and AS. When differentiating between these two categories, I ask parents about language delays. Language development is actually a strength of individuals with AS. Some believe it is an over-developed skill to compensate for early developmental problems with exploration (getting up and touching everything as a toddler). Adults with Autism might have functional speech, but always report language development delays. Obtaining speech, they tell me, can happen at the age of 4 or 5 years old or later, and with the help of relatively intense therapy.

Another difference has to do with friendships, and affiliation (wanting to be around people and be known by people) in general. Most individuals with AS tell me they really do want friends, and want close, intimate relationships. Most people with Autism, however, tell me or indicate unequivocally in some way that they couldn't care less. People with Autism do not seem to have the same drive to associate and affiliate with others compared to those with AS.

Finally, when looking just at the cognitive skills, people with Autism can have (sometimes by definition) a very low IQ or a very high IQ. People with AS, on the other hand have (by definition) an average or above-average IQ. Further, people with AS have clear dominance and non-dominance within the various skills and abilities that go into estimating an IQ score. For instance, verbal skills usually rank very high, and non-verbal skills (those that are more sensory or motor-mediated) are average or below. People with Autism, on the other hand, have a relatively even spread in skills and abilities that go into estimating an IQ (e.g., verbal and non-verbal skills are more similar in strength).

High-Functioning Autism (HFA)

Many professionals I know use the terms Asperger Syndrome (AS) and High-Functioning Autism (HFA) interchangeably. Traditionally, HFA referred to a person diagnosed with Autistic Disorder who achieves well in academics. Why academics? Academics seems to be the main way we evaluate the functionality of children. It is the area of functioning where the standards are most precise and most plentiful. The individuals I have known diagnosed with HFA have had average-to-high IQs and good grades. Social impairment is usually an issue that parents report is long-standing and resistant to therapy or other intervention. My guess is that traditional HFA diagnoses will be easily rolled into Autism Spectrum Disorders with use of the *DSM-V* and be an example of a person diagnosed with higher functioning in several key continua. This will likely further blur the distinction between

AS and HFA. In my experience, these are two separate diagnoses which mean they have two separate treatments (if intervention is warranted) and two separate prognoses or outcome directions.

PDD-NOS

Pervasive Developmental Disorder—Not Otherwise Specified (PDD-NOS) is something you might hear about or see on a neuropsychology or psychology report. NOS in the *DSM* usually means "something that almost meets categorical criteria, but not quite." Since we are dealing with a clunky Categorical System of classification (the *Diagnostic and Statistical Manual* [*DSM*] is a Categorical System of diagnosis), some presentations will almost meet criteria for categorizing, but fall short in some way. If we are certain a presentation belongs under the PDD umbrella, but does not really fulfill the criteria for a more specific diagnosis (like AS), professionals will label it PDD-NOS.

If I am working with a person formally diagnosed with PDD-NOS, I know the previous professional has left me the majority of the work to do. It is up to me to look at this individual with more of a Continuous System of classification so I can assess how I might help this person in therapy. Parents of children with this diagnosis should ask their care professionals what, exactly, this diagnosis means to them. Have them describe the symptomatology and functional deficits they are seeing, and those that need support and intervention. "What is the problem and what can we do about it?" is a good question to ask.

Non-verbal Learning Disorder

Non-verbal Learning Disorder (NLD or NVLD) is not a diagnosis recorded in the *DSM*. NLD is, as the name suggests, a learning disability. As such, it is usually the domain of highly specialized individuals working in education. The group of professionals I have found that can diagnose and offer recommendations for intervention of NLD most effectively are neuropsychologists (a specialty discipline within psychology devoted mainly to assessment) and educational therapists. Educational therapists do exactly what it sounds like they do—therapy focused on academic skills and Executive Functioning skills. However, I am sure there are many other professional disciplines that feel comfortable and competent to identify NLD and set up treatment plans.

Byron Rourke is generally considered the godfather of NLD. In the 1990s, Rourke wrote a series of publications on non-verbal learning disabilities. He described NLD specifically, and did a brilliant job of it. In his book *Syndrome of Nonverbal Learning Disabilities* (Rourke 1995), he makes a remarkable declaration when he postulates his White Matter Model as a cause of NLD. Many of you may know that the brain is composed of grey matter, or cell bodies. Grey matter forms many of the structures of the brain, such as the cortex (the top shell of the brain where a lot of information is stored, among other things). White matter on the other hand is composed mostly of myelinated axons, or the material that transmits information between parts of the brain. Rourke describes grey matter as the buildings, and white matter as the roads and other infrastructure (bridges, highways, etc.). The White Matter Model suggests that NLD is the result of various structures of the brain having trouble communicating.

In many respects, there is considerable overlap between the presentation of NLD and the presentation of AS. Individuals with NLD have problems with Executive Functioning which are almost identical to those of individuals with AS. Individuals with NLD also report problems with Social Functioning and some sensory issues. Specifically, several students I have worked with in the past report that they struggle with understanding non-verbal communication and often miss the nuances of conversations and social interactions. The overlap between AS and NLD is high, and some professionals have suggested that all people with AS have NLD as their specific learning disability, but not all people with NLD have AS.

There are some areas I look at in order to make a distinction between AS and NLD. First, individuals with NLD almost always report strength in math relative to weakness in reading. This is typically the opposite academic profile from AS (generally good in reading, not so good in math; there are, of course, exceptions to this). Second, while both groups report problems with socializing, including making and maintaining friendships, children with NLD can look more typical than teens with AS. They tend to wear more mainstream clothing and hairstyles, and their behavior is more age-appropriate than individuals with AS. One can assume that one of the main jobs of adolescence is to fit in (or not fit in in a systematic way). Since much of our social persona (how we appear to the world in both behavior and appearance) is based on what we think people are looking for, we either have to guess what people want, or copy them. Both groups (NLD and AS) seem to be equally inaccurate in guessing what people want, so it is possible that people with NLD are more successful at copying what they think is typical.

XYZ

I credit this term to Kathryn Stewart who wrote about the XYZ child in her 2007 book *Helping a Child with Nonverbal Learning Disorder or Asperger's Disorder* (Stewart 2007). The term describes individuals who have symptomatology that represents "a little from column A, and a little from column B," but not enough to achieve any distinct diagnosis. This is an important group of individuals because diagnosis drives treatment, and it also directs resources. Children who have problems with Executive Functioning, but not enough to warrant a diagnosis, are often those who fall through the cracks socially and academically. A child who has anxiety around social situations and thus trouble making friends, an ability to interpret pragmatic language but has a generally flat affect, and problems in both vocabulary and math, might be an example of an XYZ child. Another example is a child that only eats white foods, but seems to have no other sensory issue of note. Consequently, XYZ children seem to benefit (at least, not suffer) from most of the interventions designed for children with AS and NLD, and especially those designed to support EF deficits.

CHAPTER 2

ASSESSING STRENGTHS AND DEFICITS

In her book on the topic, Kathryn Stewart (2007) lists several features that are common to individuals on the Spectrum. Dr. Stewart categorizes these features as areas of strength and areas of weakness that are common to most people with Asperger Syndrome (AS) or Non-verbal Learning Disorder (NLD). Tony Attwood (1998) provides a longer exposition in his book on the topic as well. The notion of seeing these features as distinct strengths and weaknesses might soon become outdated as we see expectations for academic, professional, and social functioning change over time. For instance, dysgraphia (clinically poor handwriting) is common in people on the Spectrum, but access to technology has made handwriting less essential than it was even 20 years ago. For that reason, I will present a summary of features identified by scholars, as well as my own observations, in a more neutral format and provide examples and reasoning for how each can be viewed as an asset or a deficit.

General Areas of Strength

The following are general strengths of the Autism Spectrum Disorder (ASD) population which include certain types of memory function, verbal skills, use of technology, and adherence to ideals such as truth, fairness, and justice in dealings with others.

Memory

Individuals on the Spectrum seem to have excellent memories. They can be especially talented at information learned in a rote style, such as lists of declensions in Latin class, or the transfer stations in your local public transportation system. With some notable exceptions, information received via the auditory sense (hearing) is particularly well-memorized. This is not limited to hearing someone else speak, though. Some individuals on the Spectrum learn to present information to themselves by speaking it out loud (when alone) or subvocalizing information (when in a library) for superior recall. It is not uncommon for individuals on the Spectrum to remember whole passages of conversation in my office (that they later use against me). It is the case that all of us have a theoretically unlimited capacity for information storage, but individuals on the Spectrum seem to have better access to certain types of factual information, especially when it is organized effectively and cued properly.

Particularly effective is the process of rote memorization—or learning ordered items by repetition. In this way, one can see that one item cues the next, and so on, leading to flawless recall. Several of my students easily learn pi to the nth digit, lists of vocabulary words, or other items that can be recalled serially (one after the other in a specific order). Parents often express exasperation at the seemingly selective memory of their ASD children. They report to me that their child can remember the actor and the actor's birthdate of all of the Doctors on the television show Dr. Who, but they cannot remember the process for doing laundry, or to take a shower each morning. Consequently, remembering lists of information (implicit memory) and remembering how to do laundry (procedural memory) require two different memory processes. ASD individuals usually excel at the former.

The upside of this skill is not difficult to see. Most skilled professions require the ability to call upon large information stores. Jobs in science, technology, and history have an ever-increasing fund of relevant information. One of the best aspects of my job is the access I have to individuals who know a lot about many things. The ASD individuals I work with know definitions and origins of words (great when writing a book), grammar and spelling rules (great when editing a book), history facts, political facts, science facts, video-game facts, information on computers and technology, and the list goes on and on. I find my clients infinitely captivating and interesting because I have learned who knows what information, and what questions to ask.

There is, of course, a downside to this. Often it seems like the information is static, and these individuals can store it and recall it like an encyclopedia. Responses to questions about specific pieces of information remind me of the old internet search engines in that I can get answers to questions that clearly do not consider the context of the question I ask. It is up to me to ask questions in a specific way. In the same way, these children can perform poorly on exams if the information is accessed (via the test question) in a way that is different from how it was presented in class. The information is in there, but is inflexible and does not integrate with other stored information or experience. There also seems to be some evidence that information can be recalled associatively, if not serially. By this I mean that one piece of information will remind the child of another, which will inspire another piece of information. Discussions, especially with several individuals on the Spectrum, can depart quickly from the original topic as each individual "free-associates" their way through the conversation. In my experience, many of these discussions are unintelligible, seemingly directionless and self-focused. In class discussions I call this "tangenting" and have imposed an outright ban on it.

In social skills class, I often start out with definitions when I am teaching a concept. For instance, I once wanted to talk about "teen-angst." It was my experience that adolescents on the Spectrum do not realize that the rest of adolescent society is in a state of perpetual dissatisfaction with life. I started out by asking the students the definition of "angst," and right away they were able not only to give a definition, but also to give me the origin of the word (German), as well as common uses (like "teen-angst"). If I had let this line of reasoning go on, the teens might have pursued other German words that are common in today's English, the works of John Hughes (1980s teen-angst movie-maker), other words that mean "fear" ("angst" in German), or any number of things that were on their mind at the time. They would have free-associated for the entire 45 minutes of the class and felt much better after the experience. I was going somewhere with this, however, so I had to remain vigilant for any of these tangents and rein them in before I lost control of the class.

Parents can help their ASD children by teaching them to use their knowledge and verbal skills to enhance social interactions and conversations, and avoid being a drag on conversations. One simple way I do this is by being open and honest when I am bored in a conversation, the ASD child is offering information I did not ask for, or it is clear that the conversation has become more of a monologue than an exchange of ideas. I describe my situation explicitly (e.g., "I am bored right now," or, "I feel like you are not reading my non-verbal signs of lack of interest") and offer a solution as to how they can manage the situation. Usually, my actual message to my ASD clients in these situations is, "Either become more interesting or wrap it up." I can use such dramatic phrases because I actually do find many ASD individuals I talk to interesting, and I do want to have dynamic and thought-provoking conversations and interactions with them.

Verbal Skills

This was alluded to above, but one will notice that many individuals on the Spectrum have good-to-excellent verbal skills. Their strong verbal skills is one of the reasons Hans Asperger (1944, translated by Uta Frith in 1991) called these individuals "little professors" when they were children. Researchers suggest that, due to some perceptual preferences, tendency to be sedentary, and other factors, individuals on the Spectrum do not explore their physical environment like other children. Whereas one 18-month-old child would amble over to the china cabinet and pick up (and possibly drop) a figurine, toddlers on the Spectrum would verbally mediate this experience by simply asking "What's that?" This over-dependence on verbalization and verbal skills to mediate the physical environment may result in highly advanced verbal skills, and verbalization tends to be the dominant mode of interacting with the world for high-functioning individuals on the Autism Spectrum. Even as children, the observer will notice that the child has access to sophisticated language and not only uses big words, but uses them correctly. Many parents I talk to report being overjoyed at being able to have such conversations with their little children and fondly recall such early interactions.

Children with AS will usually outperform their same-age peers on tests of verbal intelligence and verbal skills. They typically have an excellent vocabulary, good articulation, and excellent auditory memory (see above). Reading skills will also likely be judged above average. Adults will notice that they do not have to scale down or simplify their language when talking with these children. In my experience, these individuals tend to be excellent at spelling, and can give definitions of a word on the spot (e.g., half of my 11th grade class the other day immediately gave me dictionary definitions of the word "satire"). As children, these individuals tend to prefer the company of adults rather than peers because adults are a better match for them verbally. As mentioned above, if information can be verbally mediated (e.g., if a book is listened to or even read out loud), these individuals tend to have very good immediate and delayed recall for the information. Finally, a discovery I found truly surprising is that these individuals, even as children, tend to be natural public speakers. In our school, students have to prepare and deliver a presentation on a specific topic they have researched and many are not only fascinating, but deliver brilliantly and with confidence.

High volume of word production, lots of information to share, and difficulties in telling when people are uninterested can result in people avoiding you socially and being reluctant to engage you in conversation. Some students can also get hung up on using the precise words to express themselves. Brief explanations turn into lengthy diatribes about why they are using a different shampoo. While use of literal and technical language might be high, use of figurative and non-literal language is a struggle. As children, jokes tend to stall at the level of puns and wordplay. Reading skills (decoding) are very high, but reading comprehension skills (identifying the main point, summarizing) can be low. Describing what a passage is about becomes a chore, despite near-perfect recall of the content.

It is my experience, however, that even though skills such as reading comprehension are difficult to obtain and master, they can be achieved and improved. Parents should consider reading books along with their ASD child so they can discuss the content of the book. Parents should ask their child about themes and content, ask their child what the book or a specific section from the book is about, how they know (what is their evidence from the text), and what the text says about the character's experience and feelings. It is highly recommended for parents to read books assigned in Literature class along with their ASD child in order to enhance the classroom instruction and encourage greater class participation and meaningful discourse between the ASD child and the teacher, and with his or her peers. Parents should contact the child's teacher so the teacher can track classroom behavior and evidence of improvement in reading comprehension.

I have also known students who were dependent on "discussing" information in order to learn it. A literature teacher once approached me to discuss a student she found puzzling. This student never did homework, and indeed never read the book for class, but was one of the top performers both in the class discussion and on exams. I too found this puzzling, so I observed several classes. What we discovered was that this student was not just participating in the class discussion, he was dominating the discussion. He was directing the content of the discussion so effectively that he really did not need to do any of the other work in the class (including reading the book). The information he accessed to take the exams was real and his mastery of the content was legitimate, as far as the exams were concerned. This approach to learning might have been fine if he were the only student in the class, but lectures had degraded into a one-on-one discussion between him and the teacher. Consequently, I suggested he show proof of having read the book before being allowed to speak in class. The teacher reported that his exam scores initially dropped, but class discussions were much more balanced and she felt more confident that he could maintain himself in a college-level literature course the following year.

Technology

Many AS students seem innately attracted to technology, and will report that they want to pursue a career in computers or technology. This makes perfect sense since computers are orderly and rule-based, and technology is prolific. For the individual who wants to pursue a career in technology, there seems to be an unlimited amount of information one can learn about, and the field is constantly developing and changing. This is a perfect field for individuals on the Spectrum. Ideal schools for parents to explore for their ASD students are computer-based schools where students must use computers for all academic work. Most of my students come with some knowledge of computers, but occasionally some have little-to-no computer experience. However, lack of experience has never been a problem as few take more than a week to become proficient at use of both their personal computer and our network.

The upsides to a strong interest in and somewhat innate knowledge of technology are many. Computers create an analog and often useful examples for some of the workings of the human mind. It is my experience that these children will organize their computer in a way that looks much like their mind. If they store information haphazardly in their minds, they will store it haphazardly on the computer. Not even all the processing power in the world will help them find the missing homework they know they completed, but inadvertently "hid" on their computer. On the other hand, I have found that, as an educator, working with students and their computers can have a bidirectional effect. A student who is taught how to store information effectively on a computer tends to store information more effectively in his or her brain. It would not be surprising to me that, as a student's ability to use a computer effectively as an organizational tool increases, so does their ability to store and recall information (the process actually gets faster and more accurate).

Despite relatively high consequences, students seem to be often on the internet during class. Some students are dependent on having the internet access limited on their computer in order to be successful in a school program. They desperately want to stay in the program, but cannot stop themselves from accessing the internet without permission. It seems the unlimited access to information of all kinds that is offered by the internet is too tempting for most of our students. It is not uncommon for computer and internet use to become a compulsion. With indiscriminate internet and computer use, students can download viruses, pirate media, and change settings on their computer which effectively destroy the computer and make it unusable. Again, no level of threatening will stop some of these students from tampering with their computers. Many of these students become dependent on the limitations we place on them (no internet access, leaving the computer at school overnight, always turning the computer screen toward the teacher) in order to remain in the program. If you find that your child is both dependent on the computer and internet to perform well academically, and seems unable to use the computer safely, you are highly recommended to seek out therapeutic services.

This behavior is not limited to school, it seems. We have recommended some students to have access to a second computer they can fiddle and tamper with, and leave the school computer with the parents when not in use for school work. Parents can, unfortunately, allow unlimited computer access to their child, and some of these children simply cannot both have unlimited computer/internet access and be engaged in family life or complete homework. Sleep deprivation, isolation (especially from the family), and academic failure are some of the typical outcomes I have seen for a child who cannot regulate their computer and internet usage themselves, and have parents who are unable or unwilling to do it for them.

Truth, Fairness, and Justice

Individuals on the Spectrum can place a high value on justice, truth, and honesty. They tend to be rule-bound and compliant when an appropriate argument is made for their compliance. In fact, children on the Spectrum tend to be much more compliant than Neurotypical (NT) children. Whereas the "Just Say No" campaign of the 1980s was a terrible waste of time for most adolescents as far as drug intervention was concerned, it was probably effective for adolescents on the Spectrum. An easy argument can be made for the dangers of drug use. This attention to honesty appears to go both ways as well. In school, teachers have to do relatively little policing of behavior because students are more than willing to police their peers. Parents should be aware of this because this policing behavior may be valued by teachers, but it is shunned and sometimes punished by peers. ASD children can report on all kinds of rule-breaking, and while some of them intend to get others in trouble (this does happen, but infrequently), most value the orderliness that rule-abiding provides and are motivated to maintain the order. In this regard, ASD individuals make excellent citizens. This is one of the most honest populations I have worked with and, again, if the question is asked correctly, one should expect to get the truth each time.

The value of honesty and respect for justice cannot be overstated. These individuals tend to be trustworthy and principled. As an educator, I find it is especially refreshing working with these children as they can be reasonable and open in groups as well as individual conversations. I am amazed at the kinds of things these children will admit to me. It takes very little prodding to get them to admit cheating on a test, suicidal thoughts and gestures, embarrassing behaviors (e.g., compulsive pornography use), and all kinds of other topics the NT teenager will never discuss with an adult. Individuals on the Spectrum also tend to be interested in not just what to do, but why. When learning about manners, my students often ask about why people shake hands instead of hugging. The student who gets used to appropriately asking the "whys" of a situation is more likely to become a conscientious worker who takes responsibility for his or her behavior in the workplace.

The downside to this focus on rules and justice is, especially as one grows older, that there needs to be an appreciation for complexity in human interactions. Our students struggle with the "gray areas" of society and social interaction. The line between "snitching" and being a good citizen seems to get more opaque as one ages. For instance, when some of our students have obtained their driver's license, they have learned to drive at or below the speed limit (applying the black and white of the law) while at the same time tolerating rides from their parents and friends who might drive over the speed limit, in technical violation of the law. Some of our students have been labeled as "the Sheriff" by their NT peers because of their inability to discern the gray areas, or their propensity to misinterpret what they are seeing, or their intense dependence on order and fairness. Many of our younger students reject the notion that life is not fair. Fair for them becomes the standard, and they will go to great lengths to obtain fairness. Even as teenagers they can keep count of how many turns in a game their peer got compared to them. They seem to have perfect recall for everything you, the parent, said regarding what they will be allowed to do and what they will not. Most people know that this kind of record-keeping tends to lead to frustration and, in some cases, incapacitation. There is a benefit to accepting some imperfection and injustice. Our students struggle with this acceptance.

Parents do well to acknowledge this tendency toward honesty and justice while at the same time talking about how it might be a detriment. For instance, I talk with students about what their peers might think of them when they are telling on someone, and how this might affect later interactions with their peers. I talk about being naive and easily taken advantage of by others. At the same time, I talk with my ASD students and clients about turning that motivation for justice outward and about being an advocate for someone else. We talk about volunteerism and jobs where people are paid to be advocates. We also talk about jobs where people are paid to take account of something, such as people who work for the Internal Revenue Service or bankers. If more individuals with ASD worked on Wall Street I do not think we would have had the problems we did with the banking sector years ago. ASD individuals are natural-born whistleblowers.

Special Interests; Areas of Intense Focus

Parents are well aware that their children on the Spectrum have things the mental health community call "special interests." Parents often call them annoyances or fixations. Children can demonstrate an intense focus in a specific area of interest. Everything becomes about this interest, and interests can vary from child to child. Special interests often span the fields of science and engineering (some experts suggest the focus on science is linked to a general strength in "Folk Physics," or a seemingly innate understanding of how the physical world works) and tend to be more general early in life and get more specific as the child ages. For instance, a young child might be interested in trains, and graduate to train schedules, or steam engines, as they age. Despite this being a common feature for children on the Spectrum, the intensity of the focus can be concerning for parents. Parents can worry about the restricted nature of their child's experience or wonder if the child will ever pay attention to anything besides their special interest. The special interest seems to take the place of friendships, hobbies, or other interests.

The intensity of the special interest seems to lessen over time for many individuals, and the child's experience broadens as the parents engage the child and help them explore their interest. Interests can lead to exploration within a field of study. For instance, interest in dinosaurs can broaden to paleontology or other sciences. Children can also be encouraged to research their interest, and can be trained in ways to read about and study their interest. These skills can then be applied to other fields outside the child's interest. For instance, the school where I work has a class that combines research and public speaking where students are encouraged to pursue study of their special interest and put their findings into a presentation that others will both understand and find interesting. This process opens up a host of opportunities to train children in various school skills that will help them academically and professionally.

Special interests also open up the door for specialty areas of study and professional pursuits. If an individual can navigate school and the early professional career path, the opportunities for specialization become plentiful. Loyalty, ability to memorize large amounts of information, and a special, intense interest can make for a valuable employee.

It is the case, however, that individuals on the Spectrum, especially as children, need encouragement to branch out and diversify their experience. For instance, some students in our research and public speaking class have topics which become "banned." One student was very interested in horses, and for several projects looked at the topic of horses from every possible angle. If not explicitly told to move on or find another unrelated topic, this student would have studied and presented on "horses" for four years while he attended our school. These children struggle to understand the idea that others are not as interested in their special interest as they are. They will deliver diatribes until the listener interrupts or walks away, and then find someone else to lecture on their special interest. Study of their special interest can become overly intense and exclusive, and these children will sacrifice other duties (e.g., homework, sleep) in order to continue their study. These individuals benefit from help from parents and other adults on how their special interest ties to other disciplines, bigger pictures, and how it can connect them to society.

Strengths Profile

Each individual on the Spectrum (like all humans) has an individual constellation of specific strengths. Some of our students tend to be really good at music composition, color matching, logic, prose writing, or athletics. Exceptions to rules are almost common. For instance, math tends to be the most difficult subject for our students, but occasionally we have a student on the Spectrum who excels at math. Most of our students have dysgraphia (problems with fine motor movement required for handwriting), but some have beautiful penmanship. These individual strengths do not mean that they no longer qualify for a Spectrum diagnosis. These strengths can be part of their unique contribution to the world. Thoughtful parents and skilled educators will investigate these strengths, and work to incorporate them into what eventually ensures the student's ongoing productivity and happiness.

Unique skill sets and strengths are what also make it possible for ASD children to bond with children who are not on the Spectrum. It is good to find your "tribe" of individuals with similar social and organizational needs, but it can also be beneficial to have variety in social interactions and be exposed to people not like you. Specific strengths (such as athletics) can be the "in" a child needs with his non-Spectrum peers that adds immediate credibility.

It should be noted that strengths are different from interests. Some of our students are very interested in sports (it is their area of special interest), but are not skilled in them. In a case like this, I would not recommend the child join a city sports team. We can easily predict that this would lead to ridicule and further ostracization from NT peers as the child's enthusiasm for the sport does not match his or her skill at playing the sport. Watching the ball game with Dad, or joining a fantasy football league, might be a better outlet for that interest. If a parent would like to expose their Spectrum child to the NT world and have them be around NT peers, I would always recommend following their child's strengths. It is the case that not all of the strengths of children on the Spectrum readily lend themselves to group activities, but creative brainstorming can be an effective tool in this regard. The good news with today's society is that it seems to be embracing more of the activities that individuals on the Spectrum (and especially the adolescents) find enjoyable. There are now video-game competitions, LARPing (Live Action Role Play) clubs, and RPG (Role-Playing Game) competitions in many cities. For whatever reason, children on the Spectrum seem to love (or at least be able to engage socially in) one or more of the above-mentioned activities. Intense interest in animals leads to volunteerism at the zoo, love of movies leads to Friday night movie clubs at the local theater, and so on.

Areas of General Deficit

Individuals on the Spectrum are typically identified by their limitations. There seem to be three general categories of challenge or limitation. Each of these categories deserves a longer explanation than can be given here, and where possible I will refer to other works which provide a more thorough or specific description. The three general areas of deficit are Social Skills and Pragmatic Language, Executive Functioning, and Sensory Integration.

Social Skills and Pragmatic Language

All social interactions are governed by a set of rules or norms (things people consider, by general consensus or tradition, to be normal or typical). Many social interactions are discussed, and the rules of these interactions are explicit. Most notably, people learn to "mind their manners" as a child. For example, in many societies children are taught to shake hands with their right hand, say "please and thank you," and speak with "indoor voices" when inside. However, for every rule we learn explicitly (such as manners), there seem to be about a thousand implicit rules. For instance, most people seem to know implicitly how far to stand from someone when talking to them. This distance can change based on context (e.g., inside or outside), content of discussion (e.g., personal or public), and familiarity between the individuals. Most people can move from conversation to conversation and adjust their personal space seamlessly and without thought. Individuals on the Spectrum can struggle with differentiating context and discussion content when judging personal space, and this is just one aspect of hundreds of social norms one must master to be proficient in socializing.

Pragmatic language can also be described as "practical language," or language that promotes communication of ideas and experience. Pragmatic language goes far beyond literal meaning of words (a skill at which individuals on the Spectrum excel) and into the nuances of language, which are largely non-verbal. The adage "It's not what you say, but how you say it" is referring to pragmatic language. Western society relies heavily on context and pragmatic language for communication, and English as a language is infinitely flexible. Miscommunication is especially common among individuals on the Spectrum. The mistake I hear about most commonly is an individual on the Spectrum taking a message literally when it was intended to be taken figuratively.

My assessment of individuals and families typically includes a retrospective analysis, and parents sometimes remember the social deficits emerging first. Our students tend to exhibit delays in the activities of socializing from early in childhood. When other children are moving from parallel play (playing side by side on the same activity but not interacting with each other) to cooperative play, ASD children still tend to prefer playing alone. Parents have reported that they imagine their child is lonely, but when asked to report objectively, they report that it appears as if their child seems truly content to play alone. In addition, getting the child to interact with others can take a lot of energy—so much so that parents eventually succumb to letting their child play alone. In cooperative play, these children seem especially subject to tantrums and blow-ups, and parents report that these incidents can be embarrassing.

Children on the Spectrum often report to me that they are not actually lonely, but truly content to play alone. I get the sense that they could take or leave cooperative play, and struggle to see the benefit of playing with others. They are also able to engage well with people with whom they are familiar (such as parents and siblings). Play with others can still look egocentric and repetitive. The bad news is that while these children are playing alone, their NT peers are actively and dynamically learning the rules of society. Pragmatic language (the often non-verbal language that mediates the vast majority of our social interactions and communication mentioned above) is like any spoken language—the younger you are and the more immersed you are in a society of people who are fluent in the language, the better you seem to learn and retain it.

Deficiencies in social skills and pragmatic language use start to show up when social interaction with peers becomes a major part of the child's experience and process in learning, which is typically elementary school. In kindergarten and 1st grade, the child can come across as quiet and withdrawn, but can still tantrum and be unusually rigid. Rigidity can come in the form of food preferences (eating the same thing every day) or play preferences (playing with the same toy the same way), or any number of routines. As the child ages, his peers become more sophisticated in socializing, reading, and producing pragmatic, non-verbal language, and modifying their behavior to adjust to the implicit expectations of the social environment. Elementary school is difficult for students on the Spectrum, and if the child does not receive services (e.g., social skills training, academic training), junior high school (grades 6–8, ages 11–13) can be devastating. All of the children who apply to attend our school for the higher grades have stories of being teased, especially in the middle grades. Most have terrible stories that include ridicule by adults and bullying by peers. The stories are almost always centered around school as these children (and parents) have typically learned to limit peer socializing to that which is absolutely necessary.

By high school, most children on the Spectrum are primed for an anxiety or mood disorder, or both. If I could distill the message I get from teens on the Spectrum, it would be something like, "Everyone seems to know something that I don't, and I have no idea how to figure it out." They are usually referencing social skills and pragmatic language use. Imagine if you did not speak Japanese, but were dropped in the middle of Tokyo, and instead of the normal helpful Japanese person you were likely to meet (Japanese people, in my experience, are very polite and friendly to outsiders), you were bullied, punished, and marginalized. Worse yet, no one would take the time to help you learn, so you were relegated to either continuing to make the same mistakes, or isolating yourself. Many teens who attend the school where I teach look a little shell-shocked and suspicious for about the first three months. It takes about that long of being among peers and adults who are demonstrating care and interest in them to re-learn that people can be safe.

It is my experience that all individuals on the Spectrum can improve their Social Functioning and pragmatic language skills, regardless of their age or experience. This is important to consider as so much of our lives involves social interaction. Parents I have worked with have found that the earlier they begin working on social skills and pragmatic language training, the better their children do. In a way, learning to communicate effectively using pragmatic language seems much like learning English, French, or Arabic. The earlier one starts, the easier it is to learn and the more fluent one becomes. Parents will do well to make social skills and pragmatic language training a part of interactions at home, as well as seeking out knowledgeable professionals to help in this process of learning.

Executive Functioning

I suspect deficiencies in social skills and pragmatic language use are not exclusively the result of lack of exposure or practice (as I suggested above). Intertwined in social skills are organizational skills like those associated with Executive Functioning (EF). Again, there are a lot of resources that will give expositions on EF, but here I will provide some brief context. EF includes the cognitive processes that happen to information from the time it goes into the brain (through the senses) to expression of that information (e.g., answering a question in class). It includes perception and the directing of attention, manipulation of the information (e.g., where information is eventually stored in long-term memory, how information is synthesized with other information), and forming a product (e.g., information recalled for an exam).

There are two lines of reasoning I have looked at that make sense to me, and point to two parts or processes in the brain that could explain problems in EF. First, some believe that poor EF skills are the result of poor functioning of the prefrontal cortex which is the very front part of the brain shell just behind the eyes. The prefrontal cortex seems to serve a lot of different cognitive functions, and can be further subdivided into various regions. For our purposes, it is supposed to be the most evolved part of the brain, and the structure can act as an executive assistant to the brain, and thus the body. Use the business office as a metaphor for the brain—where all the action happens. If you think about a business office, the executive assistant is the person who knows where everything is and what is going on at all times. The prefrontal cortex plays the role of executive assistant in the brain. There is some evidence to suggest that the prefrontal cortex does not work efficiently or effectively in individuals on the Spectrum for some tasks. I will discuss some of these tasks later in this section.

The second theory is called the White Matter Model, as described in detail by Byron Rourke (1995) and that I mentioned in the first chapter. White matter (as opposed to gray matter) is the term used to refer to the brain matter and structures that move information around the brain, or the infrastructure (the highways and byways) of the brain. The most famous white matter structure is the *corpus callosum*, or the big band of fibers that connects the right hemisphere with the left hemisphere of the brain. We sometimes describe people as "right brained" or "left brained," but the truth is that most of a person's experience is mediated by both hemispheres, and multiple brain structures within each hemisphere, and these brain structures need their highways for transporting and sharing information. Rourke suggests that the deficit in EF exhibited by individuals on the Spectrum is a problem with the white matter, like when the executive assistant's network is down and he or she cannot send or receive email. Structures (such as the prefrontal cortex) perform only as well as the information they have access to and the speed with which they can access the information. If the infrastructure is faulty or inefficient, the fruit is not getting to the market, regardless of how ripe it is.

The above theories are clearly a simplification of the problem in EF seen in individuals on the Spectrum. It is also the case that both theories are correct to some degree and not mutually exclusive. ASD individuals have a harder time than most with the process of planning, organizing, sorting information into meaningful groups, prioritizing, finding the main point, storing information where it can be found (recalled), and a host of activities that most people take for granted. NTs might experience these difficulties when they are stressed, tired, or hungry, but these are the daily experiences for someone on the Spectrum. Despite their often incredible intelligence and ability to memorize information, individuals on the Spectrum can perform poorly on exams because the information they memorized for the test is stored in a way that is not cued by the test question, and thus not available for recall. These individuals may not even know that the test was today. Their eyes perceived the notice on the blackboard, but the information was discarded as unimportant by the executive assistant because the brain was busy thinking about something else the teacher said just prior to perceiving the writing on the blackboard. ASD individuals can also miss the other environmental and pragmatic language cues, such as their peers organizing study groups, or discussing their anxieties about the exam.

Academic performance is an area of concern for our students, largely because of poor EF. A parent might buy his ASD child a day-planner, teach the child how to write assignments in it, and then let the teacher know the planner is in the book-bag. The teacher then takes up the mantle and helps the student, through verbal cuing, to learn consistently to write assignments into the day-planner when they are given. The teacher then cues the student to write down the date of the upcoming test, and even verifies that the student wrote the test on the correct day. Next, the teacher and the student set up a study schedule, and the teacher is confident that all the bases have been covered. The parent then forgets, that evening, to prompt the child to look in the planner at the beginning of the homework hour. It does not matter, though, because the child forgot the planner in his desk at school. Even if the communication between the parent, teacher, and student are seamless and the student remembers to study for the next exam in that class, and the student performs well on the exam, students on the Spectrum have problems with generalization (applying rules in one context to another unrelated context), so it is unlikely that these skills will help this student to study for an exam in a different class. The parent must repeat this process for each of the child's classes, and every time there is a change (e.g., holiday, new class), or it may not be applied. This is, consequently, why I encourage parents to prioritize skills because the amount of time and effort it takes to master such an EF skill can be considerable.

In my experience, many of these EF deficits can be mediated. Systems can be put in place, some tools work better than others (like computers with calendar systems with automatic reminders as opposed to paper schedules), and much of daily functioning can be simplified and made routine. It is very possible to get some control over problems caused by EF deficits, but it takes a sharp eye, out-of-the-box thinking, and a lot of elbow grease in the form of consistent repetition. Failure also needs to be part of the equation and learning process. Many professionals and parents I have worked with seem to expect that managing EF deficits is like a formula, or they seem afraid to "make things worse" or make the student upset. Every decent plan one comes up with will have a combination of things that worked and things that did not. Systematic persistence is usually a huge benefit to the child.

If there was a magic bullet for children on the Spectrum to manage their academic worlds more effectively it would have to be the personal computer. Computers have functions that can address both structural (prefrontal cortex) and infrastructural (white matter) deficits. For instance, computers can be easily programmed to remind or prompt a person to do a specific task, much like an executive assistant. I have a timer on my computer that tells me when it is time to stop writing and take a break. I used to have to gauge the quality of my writing to know when it was time to take a break. Now the computer just tells me. Regarding brain infrastructure, computers can let me create a structure for storing information which makes working with and remembering information much more quick and efficient. Computers provide a very simple hierarchy for storing (and thus retrieving) information. The potential for computers to help individuals on the Spectrum mediate their specific strengths and deficits seems endless. Computers are also highly rule-based and consistent, so they even seem to provide working conditions similar to the preference of ASD students. Depending on where one finds the roadblock between the act of directing of attention to the act of generating a product, a computer can usually be programmed to act as an intermediary.

Senses and Sensory Integration

The final of the three major areas of deficit is that of managing sensory input (i.e., information gathered from the five senses) and Sensory Integration (i.e., managing multiple inputs, selecting information, combining information). These are related activities, but I will discuss each separately.

Most of our information about the world comes by way of the five senses: sight, touch, taste, hearing, and smell. After years of experience and observation, I have come to a conclusion that individuals on the Spectrum likely have a distinctly different sensory experience than most individuals. For many ASD individuals, the auditory sense seems to be the dominant sense for gathering new information. As stated above, information heard seems to be most effectively processed and stored, and thus most efficiently retrieved (better remembered). Parents should know that a common academic intervention many of our students use is that of subvocalization. Students will read out loud to themselves, problem-solve out loud, read test questions to themselves, or any number of activities to turn what is commonly a visual experience into an auditory experience. We specifically teach children to subvocalize (speak quietly to oneself) so as not to irritate or distract their neighbors, or make people concerned about their mental stability.

Visual, on the other hand, seems to be the weakest sense. Parents should know that most classrooms were designed for visual learners. Instructions are written on the board or at the top of the exam paper, and students are directed exclusively to "read the directions and answer the questions." If the classroom teacher seems unwilling or unable to prompt a child to subvocalize, parents can train their child to subvocalize all written instructions at home and at school. This simple intervention can be a huge positive intervention for ASD individuals. Other senses offer unique obstacles and opportunities, such as touch and smell sensitivity. Certain sensory experiences can be overwhelming, and these experiences can be idiosyncratic and change as the child ages.

Interestingly, it appears as if individuals on the Spectrum have a unique experience with physical pain and discomfort relative to their other sensory experiences. I have known individuals that have had a history of pain associated with a bowel obstruction that was intense and chronic and they did not complain, and yet they could not tolerate being in a classroom when the fire alarm is going off. This might be the difference between acute and chronic pain, but sensing the fire alarm as "painful" is peculiar. Other teens wear winter coats in the summer and pass out from dehydration. I have known children who wear sweatpants under their jeans because they cannot tolerate the feeling of denim on their skin. Still other children will wear shirts and shorts in the winter, or get drenched from the rain on their way to school and are content to sit in wet clothes all day.

In my experience, a good number of children on the Spectrum are dependent on adults to help them dress comfortably and appropriately. Specifically, children need instruction about "how to dress for the weather" and the situation. Whereas some children protest at being told what to wear and how to wear it, ASD teens rarely protest when I instruct them to remove their jacket or sweatshirt when it is hot outside, but they also rarely consider the weather when dressing. They also benefit from the discussion that what feels good does not always look good. Winter coats in the summer always look strange, regardless of the brand or cost of the coat.

It is also the case that most of our experience with any aspect of the physical environment comes from more than one sense. For instance, face-to-face conversations include hearing someone speak, watching their face, and smelling their perfume. Since conversations do not (and cannot) happen in a vacuum, an individual is also sensing multiple "ambient" stimuli that are not necessarily associated with the conversation, such as other conversations, the color of the wall, or the feel of the chair. Most people's brains seamlessly integrate the information into a single feed by attending to some experiences and blocking out (and essentially "forgetting") other sensory experiences.

It is the case, however, that most people can become overwhelmed by "busy" environments. For instance, concerts were always a challenge for me as the music was loud, the stage show was opulent, people were bumping into me, and others were smoking or wearing heavy perfume. I remember my mother telling my brother and me to be quiet, and turning off the radio in the car, if she were driving to a new destination. I thought this was a strange ritual until I started driving and realized that it can take a lot of concentration to drive safely in an unfamiliar place. It is my experience that the overload threshold is lower, in general, for individuals on the Spectrum.

ASD individuals seem to benefit from a simplified sensory environment, especially if they are doing a task that requires concentration. Among the senses, visual seems to be one of the more distracting due to how difficult it seems to be for them to process that type of information. I encourage parents to visit the classroom(s) where their ASD children spend the school day and evaluate the learning environment on the following criteria. Children on the Spectrum tend to do better in classrooms that have a simplified visual field (limited posters on the wall, etc.) and are quiet (carpeted, no bells ringing or PA systems announcing news). The school where I work has experimented with seating and found that some children do best on a t-stool (a seat with one leg that requires constant balancing), and others do best with chair cushions. Children also need the ability to regulate their sensory environment themselves and the expectation that they will do so. For instance, we allow students to listen to music while doing work (and experiment with the music to find some that optimizes attention), chew gum, eat candy, stand up, or adjust their seats. Students are also encouraged to take short breaks to either wake up or calm down. The key is that the child is provided a spartan physical environment that acts as a canvas for their attention. Students then study their sensory needs and work to optimize their attentional levels for the purpose of task completion. Optimal sensory experiences are based not just on the individual, but also on the task to be completed.

Parents or teachers witnessing chronic inattention, tantrums, meltdowns, shutdowns, or blow-ups should consider the level of sensory stimulation in the physical environment. Starting with a simplified sensory environment is a good place to start when helping children regulate their attention and behavior. The child, however, needs to understand the process of calibrating the sensory environment because they will eventually be completely responsible for managing their own attention and behavior.

The primary intervention, however, is to keep the ASD child from getting to the level of being overwhelmed. Ideally, one would want the child to be able to take an inventory of their internal experience (including level of frustration, physical and mental comfort, and sensory experience) and make adjustments (take breaks, use a stress ball) before they got to overload. More likely, it will take a creative and knowledgeable adult who has experience with the child to be able to identify and point out warning signs (e.g., I have had some students get red/blush or start moaning about two minutes before overload) and situations that are likely to be stressful and overwhelming to the student. If an overload cannot be avoided, or if the plan is to create situations where the more advanced student is expected to use skills to deal with the stress, the best course of action is to let the student's system return to manageable levels on its own. I have had students spend an entire class period or school day sitting in my office in the dark, or sitting in a corner reading a book. Often, adolescents can "pull themselves together" in a relatively short amount of time (especially with practice and an informed interventionist) and carry on with their day.

Students should, however, be expected to take responsibility for their behavior in these overwhelmed/overloaded states. If the student became overwhelmed and disrupted the class, they should be expected to apologize to the class the next day. If they became overwhelmed and threw whatever was in their hands at the ceiling and a ceiling tile hit another student, they should have a harsher consequence. All students need to learn that, intentional or not, their actions have consequences. We infantilize our students by perpetually protecting them from such consequences. Their developmental disability should be seen as something they must work through and manage, not something that provides them with a pass for negative or inappropriate behavior.

Closing Thoughts

One should expect that despite fitting a specific profile or diagnosis, each individual on the Spectrum reserves the right to be the exception to the rule. This could take the form of a strength or weakness. I am aware of children on the Spectrum who are technophobes (tending to avoid computers and technology), and really have no understanding of computers. I know of others who have a complex taste palate and love trying new foods. Individuals can (and should) also change over time. ASD individuals interact with their environment, and thus change and adapt just like anyone else. The point is that there needs to be some wiggle-room for individuals on the Spectrum to be both stereotyped, and also individualistic and trend-bucking.

Strengths should be pursued as possible career paths, and weaknesses as specific intervention paths. In general, though, uniqueness should be celebrated because, culturally, most of the Western world celebrates diversity and individuality. We all have our unique contribution and way we fit into the matrix of society.

The professional community is getting better and better at adequately assessing individuals on the Spectrum. In addition, parents, pediatricians, and teachers are getting better at making appropriate referrals. More children are being correctly identified earlier in life, and thus are receiving better services earlier on. Research suggests there is a strong link between age of initiation of services (e.g., social skills training) and outcome (e.g., having friends). Like any field of health care or mental health care, professionals are limited in the services they can apply because we only see these children in a circumscribed environment. Even parents are limited in the amount of "intervening" they can do for their child because some of the skills children need to learn can only be effectively taught by peers. Instead, focus needs to be placed on education and autonomy of the individual. Parents and professionals need to begin from an early age educating their child about Spectrum disorders. From there, children need to have specific interventions explained to them, over and over, about what they are, what their purpose is, and why they work. In my experience, ASD children who take responsibility for their own learning are those that learn the most. In the same way, individuals who take the most interest in their disability and learn to self-advocate, learn how to mediate their challenges, and capitalize on their strengths, are those that tend to have the most success.

CHAPTER 3

WHY YOUR BRILLIANT CHILD IS STRUGGLING IN SCHOOL

Education in the industrialized world is steeped in tradition. For example, every child growing up in the US has heard the stories of one-room school houses on the Frontier with women in buttoned-up blouses cracking rulers and telling children to sit up straight. Each industrialized nation seems to have its own, similar story. As much as we would like to say times have changed, about the only meaningful change I can see is that one-room school houses have turned into huge school campuses with hundreds to thousands of students. Many educators would agree that a quiet, compliant child is much easier to teach to than a loud, unruly child, and they have a schedule to keep. Lessons must be taught.

There are obvious exceptions to this generalization of education, but I hear enough stories to know that most classrooms are loud. To make it easier to keep clean, floors are tiled and walls are drab. Drop ceilings do little to muffle the echo of the teacher's voice as he yells over his students to get their attention. Classrooms are old, too, because funding for education is often scarce. To further save money (or stretch an already overstretched budget), administrations reduce the overall number of teachers and increase average class sizes from 25 to 28, then 28 to 30, then 30 to 32. Fewer teachers doing more work for the same money (a paycheck the public already resents and feels they do not deserve) means tired and overworked teachers.

Add to this the fact that most adolescents are loud and brash people (we have all been there) who make bad decisions. Tired, underpaid teachers; administrators that struggle to keep a dilapidated building from falling apart; students who are programmed to do the opposite of what they are told (we call this testing limits)—this is the modern education system. This is, admittedly, a hyperbolic description to make my point. Interestingly, though, this system works (by and large) for the majority of students. It works best if students are of the majority race and culture, somewhat well-off (at least not poor), have two parents at home who have college degrees and are interested in the student's education, are Neurotypical (NT), have friends, like to learn, and are interested in extracurricular activities such as sports and choir.

Many parents will have had a bad experience with the general education system. After years of failing to jump through hoops, perhaps your child has been referred for Special Education. Special Education is usually even more costly to run than regular education, so I am sure getting those services was not easy either. Perhaps you were promised by well-meaning professionals that putting your child in Special Education would help academic, social, and organizational performance. I sincerely hope they were correct. For many of you, they were not, or not exactly, correct.

Special Education serves about 10 percent of the US student population. In the UK, about 3 percent of children have a statement of Special Educational Needs, entitling them to appropriate resources and services. Because of these services, children who 30 years ago would have dropped out of school, or been illiterate, or had unidentified mental health or behavioral problems, are now getting free specialized education. Special Education teachers are heroes to their students, and for good reason. The problem I have confronted over the years, however, is that most teachers who will work with your Autism Spectrum Disorder Child (ASD) child do not have enough specialized education to create an effective learning environment for your child.

To their credit, schools that train Special Education teachers are recognizing the need for this specialized training, and are working to develop training for teachers to work with ASD students. What these programs seem to be struggling to figure out, though, is that, under the right circumstances, ASD students can use their talents and natural abilities to excel in the classroom. Many ASD students are treated as if they are mentally retarded, but in actuality their IQs are higher, much higher, than the professionals who are placing them in classes for low-performers. In addition, the needs of a child with a behavioral disorder, such as Oppositional Defiant Disorder

(ODD), are not just different than those of a student with an ASD, often they are the opposite. The barrier to the ODD student's education is his or her defiant behavior, lack of trust of authority, or limited knowledge of the script that children use to get good treatment from adults. The barrier to the ASD student's education is one of communication, organization, and sensory issues. In fact, the ODD student can make things worse for the ASD student because of the excessive noise, movement, and general chaos that ODD children can introduce to the classroom while they are learning to get things under control.

It is not my intent to villainize the child with a behavioral disorder, or any disorder or issue for that matter. The point is that children who do not learn in the "normal" way are often lumped together in the same group. Educational systems are, by and large, designed to serve the needs of just two kinds of learners: traditional and non-traditional. The reality is that those non-traditional learners (the Special Ed children) seem to have the widest range of academic strengths and weaknesses. As I said above, I sincerely hope that if your child is receiving Special Education services, you are satisfied with those services. If not (or even if you are), the following are academic interventions your child would benefit from.

General Academic Needs

Most ASD students I work with are good at reading, but struggle with analysis and comprehension. They tend to excel at the skill called "decoding" (similar to phonics, or sounding out words and discerning their meaning based on their component parts), but figuring out what the word, phrase, sentence, or paragraph means in the overall context of the passage or book is a challenge. The talented literature teacher will try a lot of different strategies, including having the child read out loud (thus engaging the auditory sense which might be dominant), having the child make notes in the margin of the text, surveying for the main point of the chapter, or devising a schematic where the child can break each section of the text down to its component parts (activating another talent of the ASD child). Deconstruction, reconstruction, drilling, practicing, doing this process over and over until the child does it without prompting: this is the process of teaching an ASD student (and any struggling reader) to analyze a text.

Another area where ASD students can get into trouble academically is when they are required to show their work. This can be an especially challenging lesson to teach when the student can actually produce the correct answer without demonstrating the process. At times like these it is not uncommon for effective teachers to switch the lesson away from the academic content of the class and toward a discussion of the social and vocational nuances of showing one's work. ASD students often do not consider the fact that they are being evaluated not just on the product, but the process. Skilled teachers can bring up the issue that much of learning is collaborative (between the teacher, student, and other students) just like much of the work world is collaborative. Showing one's work helps everyone stay engaged in the collaborative process.

Parents tell me all the time that their child can focus on one aspect of the class (e.g., exams) at the expense of all other aspects (class participation, homework, quizzes, etc.). In addition, homework that is designed to be practice of a certain academic skill seems to be more like busy-work in their minds. It is also not uncommon for some of my ASD students to do some, or most, of the work but not all. Finally, even though the work is complete, they may not turn it in and thus get no credit for it. Following through on a task from start to finish, where "start" is reading the directions and "finish" is turning the project in is a challenge for most young students, but it seems to be a continued challenge for the ASD teen. One can make an argument that ASD students struggle to see the purpose or benefit of certain parts of the process ("It's done; why do I have to turn it in?"), struggle to see why they need to turn work in or complete it fully ("…but I understand it; why do you need to see it?"), or struggle with the concept that teachers are evaluating them, and that that matters.

Related to this, an aspect of work completion we often underestimate is that of stamina. It takes effort to do a task, and can take remarkably more effort to do our best at it when the task is boring. It takes effort to persist in an activity when we do not understand it right away. ASD students often need extra lessons in persistence, and teachers and parents should not forget the role of stamina in work completion.

There are many ways that you as a parent can help. Keep in mind several basic concepts and facts when doing homework support, looking at your child's report card, talking with a school teacher, or any of those other potentially dreaded activities associated with managing your ASD child's academic needs. First, your ASD child is smart. If there is a problem with their academic performance, it is not likely due primarily to intelligence. Also, your child is probably not any more lazy than the average teen. Third, even if those things were true, no one has ever willed themselves to be smarter or more ambitious. I encourage parents to talk with their children and their children's teachers about skills I call "school skills." Being on time to class, having materials ready for class, reading directions thoroughly, showing work (with or without a reasonable explanation as to why they should), and asking for help when needed are part of the school skills repertoire. It is more likely that your child is lacking in some school skill than that they are lazy or unintelligent.

It is the case, however, that ASD individuals struggle with motivation. They especially struggle with the developmental process of switching from external motivation (e.g., "When you start doing your homework I will stop nagging you") to internal motivation (e.g., "I will do my homework so I can feel confident for the test"). For instance, many ASD students I know do not find good grades and praise from the teacher motivating for them. Even if the teacher uses a steady diet of positive reinforcement in the classroom, many ASD students will not modify their behavior in the way a NT child would. Knowing and believing that low motivation is actually consistent with an ASD diagnosis (and having some ideas of what to do about it) has saved many parents from despair.

General Classroom Needs

For most ASD students, the rule is that the less guess-work (vague instructions, unspoken expectations, abstract concepts) there is, the better they will perform. Assessments and assignments that require forecasting, predicting, and assuming will always result in a false assessment of the ASD individual's knowledge base (unless those are the actual skills one is assessing) because of the Executive Functioning (EF) deficits that are standard with this population. Performance usually improves through direct, explicit instruction and assessment of specific skills and knowledge. It is true that this puts the onus of responsibility on the teacher to impose structure, and then communicate that structure, but it has been my experience that logical and consistent structures, taught explicitly, can be picked up and assimilated by ASD students.

Sometimes the task is about learning the structure. For example, many ASD students benefit from explicit instructions on what the terms "short answer" and "essay" mean on an exam, and what is the structural difference between the two. Most of the ASD students I work with have very specific questions about where is the line between summarizing a scholar's work and plagiarizing the scholar's work. In cases like these, parents and teachers can assess the child's ability to learn and follow a plan, but teaching lessons about structure should usually be taught separately from lessons about math or science or any particular academic content.

The same should be said about predictability. Anxiety often gets in the way of performance (this is possible for everyone, really), so if teachers are to increase academic performance, they should increase the amount of predictability in the classroom. Have routines. All students should know what to expect regarding the class structure for most classes. Teachers should not change the routine when they are teaching new material. In fact, skilled teachers over-teach routine so that they are sure their ASD students will hear the new academic material when it is being taught. Testing and assessment should be the same each time they are done (unless, of course, they are testing an individual's ability to adjust to a new testing routine). Unless the assessment somehow includes examination of how the student behaves when the routine is changed, tests should be made the same format, same length, same type-face all the time.

Routine and predictability should not be the expectation of individual teachers, though. These should also occur at the level of the school. School-wide practices in assigning homework, creating a classroom routine, defining teacher, administrator, and office support roles, assessments and their relative value in the grading process should be the norm. Parents can ask their ASD child and their child's teachers questions about the routine for when a student first enters a classroom, how much major and minor assessments are worth, who students should speak to if they have a problem with another student, and similar questions to see if their child's school supports such school-wide practices.

Skilled teachers will ask for feedback from students. Solicitation ranges from "Repeat what I just said" (for the children with attentional issues) to "Summarize this lesson in your own words" (for students with analysis issues). Good teachers will say the same thing several different ways, and then make note of the wording that makes the most sense to students. With the ASD population, the difference can be as simple as a word. Recently a student refused to respond to the question "What was the central message of this chapter?" The headteacher heard the literature teacher taking great pains to get the student to respond to a question she was certain the student knew the answer to. The headteacher popped his head in the classroom and asked the same student "What was the author saying was the central message of the chapter?" To the ASD student who vehemently disagreed with the author's central message, the second wording freed her up to repeat the author's opinion.

There are numerous stories where parents and teachers have assumed the ASD child knew what was being asked, understood the expectation, or understood a rule that everyone knows. Recently a dad was telling me he was teaching his son how to drive, and they had been at the point of actually driving on the road for several months. One afternoon before heading out for another practice, the dad said he was worried a brake light might be burnt out. He asked his son to pump the brakes while he stood behind the car. When the dad got back into the passenger seat, the son asked him what he was doing, and the dad said he had been checking to make sure neither of the brake lights were out. The son said, "There are brake lights?" Do not assume your child or student knows anything, even the obvious.

Effective and knowledgeable teachers are central to ASD student success, but there are several things families can often do on their own to enhance their ASD child's academic success, even in the classroom. One successful intervention for many organizational needs is computers. Computers, and specifically laptops and tablets, can mitigate many EF and organizational problems for the ASD population. Computers have near-infinite potential for helping students organize and remember things. Computers can be set to remind you to start doing homework, when to stop doing math and start doing literature, direct you to the specifics of an assignment, connect you to information, and so on. Computers also eliminate information lost to illegible handwriting. Computers will even correct your spelling and grammar. Computers offer people options for communication. The list goes on and on.

Of specific importance to the ASD population, computers can act as an analog, or comparison, for the brain and its processes. Earlier it was mentioned that ASD individuals can have slow processing speed, and specifically when recalling information. Part of the cause of slow processing is improper storage of information. We have all saved a file in a poorly named folder on the computer. For instance, I have a folder on my computer named "Other." If I need a file that I put in the Other folder, it is going to take me a long time to find it. Interestingly, our brains store information in very much the same way—it stores it by association. Some scientists believe that the physical representation of a memory in our mind is located physically near other related pieces of information. For example, you might think of warm chocolate chip cookies every time you think of your grandmother. These two pieces of information are not the same thing, but I always think about them at the same time. They are likely stored close to each other in my brain.

Look at the desktop or start screen of a computer of an ASD student. It is likely the case that that student's processing speed, or relative ability to answer a question quickly and efficiently (assuming the student knows the answer), is related to the relative organization of his or her desktop. If the desktop is a mess (overlapping files and folders, no discernible rhyme or reason for what is put where, general clutter, or even a very full screen with a lot of small folders in neat rows) they will be a slower processor than an individual that has a tidy desktop with folders that make sense. I have seen students, through direct instruction and discipline, go from messy thinkers to organized thinkers. Once they have the process down, organizational issues become less of an issue, thinking speed increases, and they are finally able to move on to more content-based issues when it comes to academics.

Computers are also second-nature for many ASD students. Computers are rule-based, logical, and do exactly what they are told to do. There is limited guesswork with computers. They just dispassionately compute, day in and day out, without making a big deal out of it. ASD students can usually appreciate this.

Finally, computers can store many different types of information (from the Gettysburg Address to the due date of your history paper) which allows students to relax about keeping track of pencils, textbooks, library cards, or even where they should be at 10:30 on a Tuesday morning. Students who have access to a personal computer can have a simpler life and have less stuff to carry around. Everything can be digitized these days.

General Social Needs

Safety

Most teenage ASD students I meet have experiences of not feeling safe in a classroom or at school. Unfortunately, some of their concerns have to do with physical safety. Indeed, nearly every student I have talked to has a story of being bullied, or has experienced chronic bullying. Most people would agree that children deserve to feel safe in their schools. Lots of us, however, are content to let children "work it out" when they have a scuffle. Many of us justify our lack of intervention as the natural order of things ("it's how children learn to socialize," "boys will be boys"), or similar to our own experience ("and look how I turned out").

It is true that some children can certainly work things out, get knocked down in order to learn to get back up. But teasing and bullying represent highly nuanced social activities, and most ASD teens I talk to have the same interpretation of events: they were bullied by another student (or students) and the teacher knew about it and did not help them out. Often these students interpret either the teacher or other adult as being complicit (they could have helped but did not), or see the world as a generally scary place, unpredictable, hostile. This is not how children should grow up.

So far the discussion has been about peer-to-peer bullying, but another important group to consider is teachers. Do not underestimate the ability of the ASD student to make the teacher angry. Brilliant children with lots of information, little filter, and no awareness of hierarchy ("the teacher was wrong, I had to tell her in front of the class or everyone would get the same wrong information") can make any adult, even easygoing, highly trained adults, angry. I would hope this is rare, but I do know of instances where it was the teacher picking on the ASD student. Maybe it was the case that the teacher made a joke at the student's expense, used sarcasm that the rest of the class understood, but not your child, or simply ignored or disciplined the ASD student when the barrage of questions started; but adults can also inadvertently create unsafe conditions in their classroom.

I will say, for the record, that when ASD students tell me their stories of being bullied, not all of the experiences qualify for what I would consider bullying, or even teasing. Many sound a lot like mutual misunderstandings that the teacher or another adult failed to address properly. This makes sense, too, because we are again talking about nuanced social interactions that can be hard even for experts to interpret. What I have found is that when ASD students get angry or stressed, they can interpret ambiguous or even benevolent gestures or offers to help as being hostile.

My advice in these situations is to get the whole story, from both sides. Be very careful about jumping to conclusions, but definitely respond. Requesting a conference or face-to-face discussion with a teacher is often the best place to start. I also fully support making students a part of these discussions because more than likely you will have a chance to talk about social skills, relationships, pragmatic language, and, most importantly, self-advocacy.

Acceptance

All students need and deserve to have a place they feel accepted. In many school settings, ASD students achieve a level of acceptance that is more like tolerance. No one is overtly mean to them. The culture of many schools I have visited, and especially smaller schools, supports nice and neighborly interactions, but ASD teens' peers treat them less like friends and more like buddies (by "buddies" I mean casual acquaintances, or friends through circumstance rather than choice). Teens on the Spectrum often have a hard time telling the difference between casual buddies and actual friends, so often it is up to the parents to discern. Some parents seem to be okay with the majority of their child's peer social life being managed by buddies.

Choosing buddies over friends, however, is a less than ideal situation. It is my experience that, under the right conditions, ASD students can carry their weight socially both as a friend and as a student in a classroom. Again, go back to the notion that today's schools were not designed for ASD students. That includes how children are expected to socialize and perform the social activities in a classroom. I recently had the chance to set up a "teachers vs. students" competition at our school, and needed to divide all the students into several teams. I suspected that if I asked each team to choose their own team name, we could waste the day generating ideas that would get successively more odd and inappropriate. I instead asked a group of students for a theme, and immediately one student said, "Ancient Civilizations." I asked another couple of students to name some examples of civilizations (I needed at least seven) and the group generated 20 in a single breath. From there the students came up with themes for posters, team personalities (including face paint), chants, and on and on. It was gratifying to watch all the students be able to appreciate each other's ideas, and to have the working through of a problem (i.e., coming up with a team name) be the process that served to bond students of diverse interests rather than drive them apart. Not all were experts in ancient civilizations (although a surprising number were), but all could appreciate and participate in the process. Classrooms and peer interactions need to allow for ASD students to use their knowledge and skill in a purposeful way, and teachers need to support the non-traditional style of processing and learning that ASD students can use.

When I attend conferences and workshops, talk with school professionals, or meet average individuals and talk about my job, I am gratified to see that the discussion about Spectrum disorders is moving away from the impairment associated with ASD and toward a more holistic definition and interpretation of the diagnoses. Everyone deserves to be accepted and appreciated for who they are as a person, and this includes strengths and weaknesses, interests and passions, skills and personality.

Pragmatic Language Training in the Classroom

One of the things I admire about the ASD population is that many of them can absorb information quickly and efficiently (under the right circumstances, of course—see above). For the skilled teacher with an efficiently running classroom this means that there is extra time available, and this can be used to address pragmatic language issues in the moment. Pragmatic language is often described as language used for communication. Beyond the literal definition of words (a piece of the communication process ASD students excel at) is all the rest of the pieces of the communication process our ASD students struggle with. Words change meaning based on how they are said (tone, speed, timing, etc.), when they are said, to whom they are said, and about a thousand other discrete and non-discrete communication variables. The rules are incredibly complex in any language, but English tends toward greater complexity when considering its pragmatic language rules. How one says what they say is everything in today's culture in deciding success or failure, and it is an area of communication where ASD students usually struggle.

Recently a parent consulted with me about a situation in which his ASD son called him a liar. The parent reported that his son was upset about a paper he had not completed for literature class. The parent told me that he encouraged his son to go to the literature teacher and ask for an extension. He knew that the literature teacher was fair and appreciated when students advocated for themselves, so he told his son he thought he was likely to be able to work something out with the teacher and get the due date extended. When the situation ended up not playing out the way he predicted, his son called him a liar. The parent and I talked with the teacher and found out that there were a lot of reasons his son did not get an extension on the paper. Now it was time to capitalize on this opportunity. The parent, the child, the teacher, and I had a follow-up discussion, and there were several things we talked about. All of the issues had pragmatic language at the center:

1. The paper was already late, and an extension had already been granted.

2. The teacher had specifically told the class not to ask for more time on the paper ("Just turn in what you have…").

3. In advocating for himself, the student interrupted the teacher while she was talking to another student.

4. The student did not ask, but used a tone that suggested he was demanding.

5. The student (falsely) claimed he had been told he could have an extension if he just asked.

6. The student walked away from the teacher while she was still talking to him.

7. The student called his parent (the person trying to help him, also an adult) a liar.

8. Being granted an extension is never a sure thing, but the student was told that asking often improves one's chances of receiving over not asking.

Because I knew this teacher, and because this student had similar pragmatic language misunderstandings in class, the teacher felt comfortable taking the first part of the next class to address the pragmatic language issue that pertained to the class. The teacher skillfully described the scenario to the class in a way that helped the original student avoid additional embarrassment, but made the discussion useful for all students. She used terms including "pragmatic language" and "misunderstanding" and avoided any shaming comments. She also talked with the student before-hand and told him that this would be discussed in class as a way to benefit other students. Interestingly, the discussion naturally turned into a larger discussion on manners (the children latched on to the part about not calling your superiors "liars"), and the entire class went by without any of the academic content being taught. This is a perfectly reasonable use of time, though, as the pertinent issue was one of communication and pragmatic language. The content is easily taught, but the skilled teacher is constantly in search of moments to teach pragmatic language. The skilled teacher and parent knows that how one says something means everything.

For his part, the parent told his son that he was wrong factually in calling him a liar, and he was also wrong socially. He talked about the pragmatic language of the term liar. He talked about its literal meaning, and then went beyond that to talk about what it means when you call someone in authority over you a liar. The parent banned use of the word in the house and in family conversation due to the fact that it was being used with increasing frequency by his son. The parent also described to his son how he could make it up to him and repair the relationship. The consequence included doing something nice for the parent (like taking out the trash when it was the parent's turn to do it) and watching a TV show together that the parent chose.

General Sensory Needs

If I could make one recommendation to parents when advocating for their ASD child in terms of sensory needs in the classroom, it would be to let them listen to music while working independently. I have confirmed that this can be written into an Individual Education Plan (IEP) if a parent asks for it. Teachers and parents should teach their ASD child to manage their own sensory environment, and start with the auditory sense. Teach them that they cannot always control the level of noise around them. In fact, insist that they have no right to tell the person next to them to stop tapping, or moving in their seat, or whispering under their breath. Tell your ASD student that these are strategies their fellow students might be using to regulate their internal environment and level of focus. Instead, teach them how to control their own level of focus, and start with headphones.

A pair of high quality, noise-canceling headphones can be a godsend to the distracted student. I have heard two reasons why schools do not want their students using headphones:

- Headphones and music are too distracting to students.

- If one student gets to wear them, every student will want to wear them.

What I say to both concerns is if it does not work, do not use it. If the headphones and music lead to greater distraction, then it is not a good intervention. If it is a good intervention (I assure you, if done properly, it is a fantastic intervention), then why can't other students use it? Teach the student to use the headphones and music only when working independently (and definitely not during lectures or when they need to listen to what other people are saying). Have them experiment with different kinds of music and sounds. Music with lyrics can be distracting, but instrumental music, or even white noise, can lead to intense levels of focus. Teach your student to use the headphones as a tool for learning and productivity, not as an entertainment feature.

Otherwise, the ASD student tends to benefit from a quiet, low-stimulation classroom. This is not just the absence of loud students constantly shuffling their feet or talking out of turn. It means classrooms with carpeted floors, no bells signaling different parts of the day, and fire alarms that are only sounded when there is a fire or fire drill. Parents and teacher will find that ASD students might not habituate to the hum of fluorescent lights, air conditioning fans, or traffic outside and report these as major distractions. Many of these are also distractions at home for ASD students when trying to concentrate on homework.

The ASD student also benefits from more space than other students might need. Many of these students have tactile issues and find knocking into other students to be distracting or uncomfortable. The more personal items the ASD student has, the more they will need to spread out, the more physical space they will need. A teacher can either give them more than one desk, or limit the number of things they are allowed to bring to class. It should also be noted that, due to occasional hygiene issues, the ASD student can smell bad and be unaware of or unconcerned by how they smell. Teachers can either keep a can of spray deodorant in their desk (this is what I do, by the way), or give their ASD student adequate space and never interact with them one-to-one (which the ASD student might prefer). Finally, the ASD student sometimes loves to do full body stretches (it seems to be a sensory re-set) that reveal plenty of underwear and flesh. Again, the teacher can either give the student plenty of space so the student is not knocking things over or putting his hands in the face of his classmates, or teach the student just not to do the body stretch. I prefer the latter (save the stretching for private) because the full body stretches can draw unwanted negative attention and be a nuisance to peers.

Everybody knows what a coffee break is. I make a point to take a coffee break, whether I feel like I need one or not, at least once a day. I have also trained myself to drink a lot of water right before staff meetings. This way I am forced to take a break to use the bathroom at least once during these marathon meetings. When I am tired and unfocused and I attend a chaotic staff meeting where teachers and administrators are having a hard time taking turns, I can become unruly and distracting. Forcing myself to step out and take a break has probably saved my job on several occasions.

Teachers should teach their students (who are more likely to become dysregulated than the average individual due to the documented sensory and stamina issues) to take breaks. At parental request this can be written into an IEP. The school where I teach allows students to request a five-minute break at any time throughout the day. Teachers must give permission, but if permission is granted, the student has five minutes just to self-regulate. They cannot go to use the bathroom (that is called a bathroom break, and should happen between classes), but they can use the bathroom to splash water on their faces (if they are tired), take several laps around the courtyard (if they are getting too worked up), meditate, deep breathe, say hello to the school secretary, and so on. The only rule besides "follow school rules" is "be back within five minutes." This is an incredibly useful strategy for regulating one's internal environment, energy level, and emotions. I know students find it useful because they almost always respect the five-minute rule. Students who go longer than five minutes lose this privilege for a time. Once they get it back, they no longer take more than five minutes.

People often ask me how realistic it is to teach children that they can stop what they are doing whenever they want and take a five-minute break. First, it is the job of teachers to help students manage this break. Teachers can deny the break, and they then explain why. They can ask students to wait, limit the number of breaks they take, or even encourage them to take more breaks, for example. In this way students learn the rhythm of the classroom, which nicely applies to professional settings outside school. Second, how often are you unable to take a break when you really need it? I have found that I need to take more breaks during the day than I usually do take. When I get up and walk around and chat with my co-workers, and then sit back down to work, I find I am more focused and productive. Teaching ASD students to take breaks, and how to take them effectively, is an adaptive skill. Most importantly, we are teaching them to take responsibility for their own internal environment and focus.

The Hill to Die On

Every parent I talk to is looking for the absolute best for their ASD child. Above I have described some ideal situations and scenarios to support an ASD child's academic needs, classroom needs, social needs, and sensory needs. It is unlikely, however, that you will find an environment or institution that can provide all of these things, in the exact way your child needs them, all the time. The quest to find such a place, however, seems to occupy the thoughts of many parents with whom I have worked.

Parents and professionals, myself included, struggle to find the balance between encouraging the ASD student to persevere, and modifying the challenge. Some decisions are easier than others. For instance, some ASD students have problems with perception, focus, and anxiety which make a skill like driving a car nearly impossible to master. In cases like this, I usually do not insist the young person learn to drive. Some ASD students have chronic sleep issues and need to use medication and behavioral strategies to ensure a good night's sleep. For those students who have sleep issues and want to sleep in every morning, the answer is a pretty easy "no." No one will tolerate an adult who gets out of bed only when they feel like it. Sleep issues aside, one needs to get out of bed in the morning.

Other issues are not so clear-cut. Also, the task of making an ASD student do something he or she does not want to do can be arduous and draining. "The hill to die on" (meaning an issue that you choose to address because addressing it, while difficult, is so important) is a phrase I hear more now than I ever did before working with this population. Be that as it may, I have met plenty of ASD students who were performing well below their means in areas such as self-advocacy, organizational skills, behavioral inhibition, cognitive or physical stamina, or other academic skills because adults had systematically modified away all the challenge out of their lives. Somewhere along the way, an adult had decided that the task was too great, or their own ability to encourage a goal had diminished, or their child was simply too impaired to meet the expectations being placed on them. If this is you and you are a parent or a teacher of an ASD student, I would encourage you to change how you think about your child or student. All of us need someone in our lives who believes we can do better, and who will support and encourage us, and ultimately hold us to a standard when no one else will. You need to be that person to your ASD child.

CHAPTER 4

WHAT SHOULD YOU EXPECT FROM YOUR ASD TEEN?

The Upside Down House

Different cultures have different rules about how parents should interact with children, and the child's role in the household. Baumrind (1966) was notable for categorizing parents in one of four parenting styles (authoritarian, indulgent, authoritative, negligent) based on how responsive or demanding parents were to their children. *Spoiler alert:* modern society appreciates the children of authoritative parents (high on warmth, high on expectations). Anthropologically, modern society goes through waves of parenting fads. It used to be the case that parents were told to focus only on their child's successes (forgetting their failures, helping the child to avoid things that were too challenging). This was the age of "Everybody gets a trophy." What we found, in short, is that we raised a generation of quitters. Life inevitably got hard and adults rarely get trophies. In fact, the older one gets, the less appreciated they become (usually).

In my practice I have learned to identify the upside down house. This is a child-centered house that operates in service of the child's or children's desires. Child-centered, however, is different from child-oriented. Child-oriented homes have covers on the electrical outlets, designated dinner times, trips to the park, and promote education. These are all things that children need in order to grow up well. The child's needs are not always in line with the child's desires. Parents should be very careful about fulfilling the desires of the child for two reasons. The first is developmental. Children are in the process of learning the concept of delayed gratification. The original work by Walter Mischel and colleagues (1972) on delayed gratification has been replicated and expanded to demonstrate a strong link between delayed gratification and a host of benefits later in life such as academic success and social competence. Children need our help to practice and incorporate delayed gratification. They need to learn that they cannot have all of their desires fulfilled as soon as they have them. The second reason is experiential. Children are naive and inexperienced. They make bad decisions all the time. They depend on a parent (with significantly more life experience and factual information) to help them make decisions.

The upside down house is focused exclusively on meeting the desires of the child. Parents in this house may be working hard to meet the needs of the child, but when one opens the doors on meeting a child's desires, demand to meet desires can overcome the demand to meet the child's needs. Examples of events and practices I have seen in the upside down house include parents who make two meals at dinner time (one for the Autism Sprectrum Disorder child and one for the rest of the family), capable children who do not contribute in any meaningful way to the running of the household, children who chronically disrespect parents and other adults, parents who drive children around who could otherwise drive themselves or take public transportation. Worst of all, the upside down house engenders a social environment where parents find it easier to dislike each other, disagree a lot, and are dissatisfied with their marriage.

The upside down house needs professional help, in most cases. The families I have worked with have no context or understanding of just how disordered their lives have become. I have worked with a number of highly educated, highly influential parents who would be embarrassed to show their clients or constituents how they run their house. How does the upside down house come about? No one I have worked with has ever chosen it. In most cases I hear stories of minor compromises that add up and get out of control over the course of years. Parents also tell me about children who, diagnostically, do not understand the burden they are placing on the household through their special meal requests and rides. Most parents I talk to are simply tired of the mental wrestling match of trying to please everyone all the time. They note struggles in and out of the home and often take opportunities to create peace wherever they can get them. It is the choice of a thousand compromises and special requests that makes the upside down house.

You might be living in an upside down house, or you might just be looking for some standards for your child who has defied all published developmental standards. You might also be wondering if the years have worn you down and you are letting your child get away with behavior that is more a representation of the culture of his or her adolescence (e.g., poor attitude, self-centered) and less about his or her diagnosis or ability. Read on.

Teen Domains

Adolescence is a tricky time to stay alive (note, I said "stay alive" and not "be alive"). At no other time in our lives will we have the greatest potential (adult-sized bodies) with the greatest amount of restriction and the least amount of freedom. On top of that, it is developmentally appropriate, as a teen, to test boundaries and break rules. Parenting teens is tough, but being a teen is a challenge in itself. Despite the limited influence (relative to potential) and responsibility that most teens have, there are several areas where they can exert great influence and be highly dependable and consistent.

Top on the list of teen domains is academics and vocational training (preparing to be an adult that meaningfully contributes to society). When I was in high school and college my dad used to tell me that my job was to go to school. That meant I would be evaluated not just on how well I did at school (behavior, grades, social life, etc.), but on my ability to get better at school. My parents were interested in grades only as a single measure of progress. They knew that certain things were hard for me, and I would likely score low, but they expected me to continue working at it and getting better. My mother would tell me that her definition of success was if I turned out to be an adult she would want to spend time around. Our goal for our teenagers should be to prepare them to be healthy and productive adults. They will spend much more time being adults than children anyway.

It should be noted that as a society we place a high premium on grades. I do not have to tell most parents, however, that there are many other ways to measure academic competence and progress. Even though I know this is hard for most parents, I would like to encourage you to place grades in their proper context. They are simply one measure of success. You may have to retrain yourself to look at other measures, such as how much your child likes attending school, positive (or, at least, non-negative) assessments of teachers, keeping better track of assignments, or being more consistent with work completion.

Academics is a tough domain for ASD students to take control of and responsibility for because, as was said in Chapter 1, most academic settings were not designed with the ASD student in mind. Ask yourself these questions: Is your child exerting effort in school? Is your child finding ways to challenge himself in the areas where he excels? Is your child avoiding challenge or hardship? Does your child blame the hard stuff on his or her teachers? ASD students need a lot of help thinking about school like a job. They need help remembering that they are constantly being watched and evaluated, that there are multiple methods for determining success or failure, and that good effort, in most cases, is preferable to good grades. Life does not get easier as one gets older, but we can certainly get stronger. Regardless of your child's disability, they can always build fortitude and grit; they can always work to get better at whatever it is they are attempting. Questions about whether you are pushing your ASD child too much or too little can be directed to knowledgeable adults that work with your child, such as a school teacher you trust, or your child's therapist.

Another domain where ASD teens can exert influence is in the functioning of the house and the household. I am not aware of any teen that enjoys scrubbing a toilet, or cleaning up after a dog, or putting dishes in the dishwasher. But enjoying an activity is not a prerequisite for its need to get done. Too many ASD teens I work with contribute little or nothing to the running of the house. They have no chores and no weekly or daily ways they are expected to keep the house neat, clean, or safe. Some of them are limited to the responsibilities of keeping "their space" (e.g., their bedroom) clean, and most do not do this reliably. My rule for parents is that expecting the ASD teen to clean up after themselves (keeping their room clean, putting their dishes in the dishwasher, hanging up their towels, doing their laundry, etc.) should be the minimum expectation. If you messed it up, you should fix it. I also encourage parents to not refer to the child's room in any way that suggests you believe it is the child's property. This can set up lines of demarcation and a sense of propriety that will be a hassle to challenge in the future. Instead, talk about stewardship. "This is my [the parent's] room that I will let you use as long as you live here. Treat it, however, as if it is my room." I push this last piece (stewardship over ownership) because it is truth. Your ASD child does not likely have an appreciation or deep understanding of the fact that the house, and thus his room, is not his property. For this reason, any time you enter his room, for any reason, this will be seen as a violation.

For instance, I have worked with several ASD children who have created a health problem in their room. They do not clean, or pick up after themselves, and the things they leave lying around, such as food, dust, moldy clothing, and, in some cases, waste, have made the room unsafe for them. The parent of the "ownership" model now has a decision to make—intrude on the child's property or further risk the child's health. This is an extreme example (though it actually happens more often than you might think), but it is completely moot under the stewardship model. The idea of room ownership has also been a slippery slope for many ASD teens. Teens who "own" their room also tend to own the computer you bought them, the phone you bought them, and the internet connection you pay for. Placing restrictions on these now becomes a fight over freedom and tyranny. All of this is avoidable by simply going with the truth.

Your expectation for your ASD child's contribution to the family should go beyond doing the minimum. I recommend that children are responsible for cleaning up the messes of others. For instance, they should be responsible for cleaning the guest bathroom weekly, and/or vacuuming the living room weekly, and/or taking the trash to the curb. It is very important that ASD teens go through the act of doing these chores as it will promote a sense of ownership, participation, and belongingness to the community (in this case, the family).

Finally, an ASD teen should have some sense that they should contribute to the overall well-being and mood of the family. It is possible to do one's chores, perform well in school, and still be a difficult person to be around. In addition to personal mood and attitude management, we all participate in corporate (e.g., at the level of the family) mood and attitude management. This expectation can be a little more challenging to describe to an ASD teen, but it looks something like treating parents not only with respect but appropriate levels of affection. I worked once with a family where the parents made a point to tell me that their son never said goodbye when he left for school or hello when he came home. As well as being polite, greetings and salutations contribute to the identity and well-being of the family (e.g., the tone and manner with which someone says "good morning" at breakfast conveys information about how they are feeling that day). In the case above, the parents had to insist that the child check in with them, say hello and goodbye at least once a day, and hug his mother in public whenever she requested it. ASD teens need to know that how they treat the members of their family is as important as completing certain chores. That treatment often stems from the values the family holds.

Power of Failure and Struggle

Many ASD students and their parents out there will have struggled with the concept of failure. What is the correct response when something seems too hard to accomplish? What should a parent do when nothing they try can get the child to meet some standard they are holding on to? This section is not about how to answer those questions. It's about making a case for letting your child struggle, face hardship, and ultimately, at times, fail.

Failure is not a consequence of lack of effort, or low skill or ability, or even of disability. Failure is a fact of life. Failure represents adventure and ambition. In my experience, parents of ASD children are keenly aware of the fact that living with a Spectrum disorder in a Neurotypical (NT) world is a great challenge. It can seem, at times, as if everything is a struggle, everything is hard. I know that it is a tough decision for parents to allow the struggle to continue with the ultimate result of failure when it is a struggle and failure they can help their child avoid.

There is always a place and time for rescue (children who can depend on their parents for such rescue tend to have more stable and warm relationships with them and others), but I would like to make a case for the potential benefit of struggle and failure. When struggle and failure result in a person feeling less safe, less capable, or having fewer options, we can question its utility. But struggle and failure are not inherently bad things. Both can make for stronger, more determined, and ultimately more victorious individuals. Here is the formula: failure, plus a nurturing parent or other adult, makes for a stronger child. Parents and adults who take the time to process failure and sympathize and encourage through struggle tend to produce children who become stronger and more determined adults. Struggle and failure are unpleasant, but they are not bad, nor are they punishment. The ASD teen really does benefit from struggle and failure, too.

Benchmarking

I was once invited to speak on preparing for post-high school transitioning for individuals on the Spectrum. I was given an hour to speak and was asked to address a few points specifically in my speech. As a challenge, I decided to see if I could come up with some developmental benchmarks for ASD students. I knew well the developmental milestones for children and adults, and I also knew that individuals on the Spectrum tended to miss those milestones by about five years, on average. To my knowledge, however, no one had come right out and set some specific standards for individuals with an ASD. I am sure it is a combination of lack of reliable information and compassionate understanding that these children really do not need another set of standards to fail to meet, or ones that are so easy they are a slight. After all, these individuals do not develop at the same rate as Neurotypicals (NTs), but they are definitely not static individuals unable to learn and grow.

The following is something of a "necessary but not sufficient" guide to growing up with a Spectrum disorder. Rather than milestones (suggesting some objective standard of functioning), I will talk about benchmarking, which suggests comparison to a standard. In this case, the standard is independent, productive, adult living.

Since this book is for parenting ASD teens, the benchmarks will start with the end of 8th grade (age 12–13). As a side note, I do not want parents of a late-diagnosed child (diagnosed after the age of 12 or so) to read what I am writing and feel like they are already too far behind. My message to all well-meaning but confused and exasperated parents is to see my benchmarks for what they are: a guide, a line in the sand, a marker flag. I will tie them to a particular age because, like it or not, most children are expected to be done with school and move into the adult world around the age of 18. Eighteen to 20 seems to be the "transition years" for most teens, so I will use that as an anchor and work backward from there.

By the End of 8th Grade (Age 12–13)...

A lot of individuals on the Spectrum report problems with regulating arousal or internal alertness, but by the end of 8th grade, ASD children should know how to regulate their arousal in ways that do not make them look strange or unsophisticated. "Self-stim" behaviors is the common term used for things like hand-flapping, pacing, galloping, or any other gross-motor behavior that appears to be out of context. The lay person is likely to have experienced seeing a 10-year-old in the grocery store jumping and flapping his or her hands. The grocery store is an excessively stimulating environment with a lot of visual, auditory, olfactory, taste, and tactile experiences. Jumping and hand-flapping appears to help the child "regulate" himself, or return to his basal arousal (a "functional" level of alertness where one is neither too alert [anxious, keyed-up] nor too under-stimulated [drowsy, sluggish, or foggy]) after being over-stimulated.

It is very human to self-regulate, but if your child has an obvious, gross-motor self-stimulation strategy that makes him or her look strange, that should be replaced with more subtle strategies by the time he or she completes 8th grade. Deep breathing and muscle relaxation are some of the public strategies that seem to work well for our children and are more subtle. Teaching a child to excuse himself to the bathroom to do stretching, push-ups, or any rhythmic gross-motor movement (safely) is an acceptable strategy as well. Often our students' self-stim behavior includes a vocalization component.

It is hard to moan or grunt in public without that activity making one look strange. Loud and physically large stretching and yawning are also popular with ASD children. Children should be taught to avoid this behavior when others are around because of the tendency to intrude into other people's space and show a lot of skin (especially their stomach) when stretching. It also tends to make them look younger than their actual age.

Why would I pick out this behavior? These self-stim behaviors are at the top of my list of reasons your child has difficulty making friends, and why making friends may continue to be hard if they continue with them. These self-stim behaviors make your child stand out in a negative way and generally look strange and unsophisticated. Children should save behaviors which appear strange for home when they can perform them in private. Parents can help their child learn new, more subtle (and, in some cases, more effective) ways to regulate arousal. Switching from an acute strategy (managing arousal when feeling out of balance) to a more daily strategy (getting sufficient sleep, daily exercise, daily meditation, manageable environment) can be life-changing for these children. Making self-regulation a daily activity and having subtle strategies to use when necessary are what all people need, but will be especially important for individuals on the Spectrum.

In addition to being helpful in socializing, minimizing these boisterous self-regulation strategies can help the child benefit more from the classroom experience. The average classroom is designed for quiet, measured interactions between students and teachers, and students and their peers. Children who master the predictable and acceptable standards for classroom behavior tend to get more teacher interaction and attention.

I am an advocate of delaying (saving for later to perform in private) or replacing these self-stim behaviors. Hand-flapping can be replaced with gum chewing. Trampoline at lunch can be trampoline before bed. I teach our students the process of "compartmentalization," or putting frustrations away until they can be properly dealt with. Interestingly, I have found that individuals on the Spectrum seem to be able to compartmentalize better than their same-age NT peers. I also advise my students to "bottle up" their feelings until they get home, or until they can get to my office.

"Please, come cry and get under the chair in my office," I say. This gradually teaches them that this behavior is okay under certain circumstances and in certain contexts. They are happy to comply because I have taught them the social consequence of climbing under the table in their science class. By the end of 8th grade, all of these behaviors which make your child appear strange to other children should be addressed. You may feel like you are working in that direction, but I will tell you that the longer you take, the more your child will ostracize himself or herself. It is also recommended that you speak with a professional about how to do behavioral delay or substitution if you are having trouble with this process. Some of these behaviors are complex and habitual and an experienced therapist (e.g., a psychotherapist or occupational therapist) will be able to do a behavioral analysis and offer the best advice and guidance.

Most parents I speak to have problems differentiating between behaviors that need to be modified and behaviors that are part of the child's personality and need to be tolerated or preserved. There is no set answer for how to decide which is which, but the goal of this process is moving toward greater independence. Which behaviors support independence and which support dependence or isolation? Also, do not underestimate the ability of all individuals to adapt, change, and be happy. I tell parents that I am comfortable rejecting the notion of the intractable behavior, or that people cannot change.

By the end of 8th grade, your child must be able to accept help from adults. Competent, knowledgeable adults tasked with the job of helping your child (e.g., teachers, clergy, other parents) are more than happy to help your child, but some children on the Spectrum refuse help. Some of the reasons I have heard may be related to sensory issues. Children sometimes do not like anyone getting too close to them. Adults tend to wear strange and pungent scents. Some adults tend to get very close to children when reading over their shoulder or in an attempt to make eye contact. Some behavior management techniques (especially those used with children with attentional disorders) encourage adults to touch children on the arm or shoulder when giving instructions.

More often, however, I hear children (ASD and NT alike) refuse help in a way that suggests they think they can do it on their own. "I know, I know, I know..." is a common response, or some suggestion that they want to try it on their own. It is occasionally the case that adults are too willing to step in and help when the real task for the child is to figure it out on their own, but many children on the Spectrum have trouble deciphering when it is time for independence and when it is time for help, and then not interpreting that help as a failure. Children on the Spectrum sometimes need practice learning to trust a trustworthy adult (like their teacher). Accepting help from others at this age can form the foundation for later skills in self-advocacy and independence.

Finally, if your child has any significant mental health issue (e.g., depression or anxiety), services should be in place to effectively address this by the end of 8th grade. If you suspect that your child has a problem with anxiety, they should be assessed by a professional right away. Individuals on the Spectrum appear to experience a very high rate of anxiety disorders relative to the general population. Depression also seems to look a bit different in this population as well. I have surmised in the past that the reasons for this different "look" to mood disorders might be related to expressive language disabilities (e.g., these students have trouble expressing both verbally and non-verbally that they are depressed). Psychologists and psychotherapists seem to be the most effective professionals at identifying and treating (or making appropriate referrals for treatment) children on the Spectrum when it comes to mental health issues. One caveat to this is that the psychologist must have experience in working with this population. Not all of the mental health treatments that are effective for this population are standard or traditional. Please ask your care provider to describe their experience and expertise with this population (especially children on the Spectrum), and then go with your instincts. You know your child the best at this point. In my experience, parents seem to have a good sense for when they feel some skepticism about their child's care provider.

Mental health concerns can sometimes be long-term, or even life-long, but treatment for them should start during the middle schooling grades. Why this deadline? The later school years represent a new set of social and academic challenges, and your child's stress is likely to increase. Stress seems to be a universal trigger for mental health symptomatology. If your child has an anxiety disorder, the increased stress that comes while studying in the higher grades will likely make it worse and your child needs to have services in place for support. Lastly, the right school placement should lead to an overall reduction in anxiety symptoms, even without direct treatment.

By the End of 10th Grade (Age 15–16)…

By the end of their 10th grade year, your child should have daily chores at home that extend beyond cleaning up after himself or herself and involve managing shared space (e.g., kitchen, living room). Your child should have mastered by now the act of cleaning up after themself. It is okay to remind your child to do this, but you should not have to say it more than once very often. Your child's bedroom (or unshared space) is a separate issue. I would not expect your child to keep his or her unshared space spotless. It should be sanitary, but can be disorganized. It is, after all, their sanctum. For most children, insisting they keep their room spotless at all times is a long, uphill battle for a parent and will take significant time and energy.

Outside of the bedroom, your child should already be taking dishes to the sink or dishwasher, throwing trash away, cleaning up spills, and moving all belongings to their bedroom (book-bag, clothing, etc.). The benchmark I mentioned above, however, includes the act of cleaning up after others or managing shared space. They should vacuum the living room, empty the dishwasher, or walk the dog. It is important for them to clean up messes or manage disorder they did not create. This is a very practical way for ASD children to learn to be a part of a community. In this case, they are actively contributing to the maintaining of the family and building a sense of belongingness. Unless you insist, ASD children have a very difficult time working for a sense of ownership and belongingness to groups.

Parents sometimes ask me why I encourage daily chores, and if weekly chores can substitute. Daily chores are easier to remember, and tend to be more manageable tasks. They do not have to re-grout the tub each day, just wipe down the bathroom sink. The tasks should become more involved as they age as well.

When working with families who have a child on the Spectrum, I often find that much of the family activity is in service of the child on the Spectrum. If plans get changed, it is usually in favor of the Spectrum child. Parents excuse obnoxious or rude behavior, clean up after children who can clean up after themselves, and other activities. I have written above that I find it especially fascinating to see adults who broker million-dollar deals or pass legislation in their professional career become completely powerless when it comes to negotiating with their child on the Spectrum. The problem is that the concept of compromise is challenging for ASD children to understand, and when they are upset, they can be difficult to live with. ASD children can make reasonable people do unreasonable things. Chores are a practical and fundamental way to recover some control and authority.

By the end of 10th grade, your child should have a regular homework routine, and need no more than one reminder to commence the routine. In order to get to the one-reminder-or-less policy, focus first on the routine. Homework should occur at the same time every day, and should occur in places that are conducive to completing homework. You may have to work with your child to find such places, and set up a schedule that works. It is the case that some people study best with silence, and others with some background noise. How do you know what is best for your child? The product will tell you. If they are getting work done, then that is a good place to study. If they are not, identify the barrier and eliminate it.

If homework time is predictable, productive, and under the child's control, getting to the one-reminder-or-less rule will be much more simple. It is not uncommon for ASD children to initiate their homework routine once it is established, and once it is clear that it is a priority for you (even if not for them). These children do, however, have organizational problems as a result of being on the Spectrum, so one reminder is perfectly fine. If you can be replaced by a sophisticated alarm clock, then you have done your job. If you must nag, keep working at it.

Some parents will find that their child is not motivated by work completion (a sense of accomplishment) or improved grades. These motivators are actually more common in adults, and not as common in teens. But without these motivators, some parents can really struggle to find a way to motivate their children to do something (homework) they do not want to do. This can be a good time to talk to your child's therapist and ask for ideas. Mostly, I would say to parents that if what you were doing was going to be effective, it would have worked by now. Try something different.

Your child should be able to find out what their grades are at any point in the school year. More sophisticated schools post grades online and children can get daily feedback on grades. Some students will have to ask each individual teacher what their grade is in their class. By the end of 10th grade, your child should be working on the skill of self-evaluation as well as being aware of how others see and evaluate them. It is not uncommon for me to question a child about their grades, and have them "estimate" their grade and be way off. Whenever I get a chance, I go right to the database and look at the grades with the teen. Another is to go directly to a teacher with the ASD teen and have the teacher comment on the child's performance. Children on the Spectrum are notoriously bad at self-evaluation in that they both overestimate some skills and underestimate others. The way you and I know how we are doing is by managing the feedback we get from others. These students do not manage this feedback effectively without help.

It is nearly impossible to set and achieve useful and meaningful goals if you are unable to accurately evaluate where you are succeeding and failing. If we cannot evaluate ourselves, or manage feedback from others, we will accomplish nothing. Checking grades and monitoring them on a routine basis (weekly, every other week) is a good first step for ASD teens to improve their academic, social, and Executive Functioning (EF) skills and performance.

Added to this, if your child sees a low grade in a class, by the end of 10th grade they should be able to figure out the next step toward improving it. Students can almost always improve their academic performance and grades by checking for missing assignments and low assessments, and increasing study time. But the easiest, most effective, universal, and functional skill you can teach your child is when and how to talk to the teacher. By nature, good teachers are motivated to help their students learn. This skill will never go out of style and will lead to a higher grade nine times out of ten (if your child actually follows through with what the teacher tells them to do, that is). This activity also provides them practice in talking with and receiving help appropriately from adults and other authority figures.

As an aside, it would be nice if you and your ASD child could identify another way to gauge progress in addition to grades. Grades do not always directly reveal progress in EF or organizational skills, at least not right away. Many ASD students are lacking some of the foundational skills necessary to do well in school, and can work and labor and see very little movement in their grades. Building better study routines, completing more of the exam in the specified time, more effective note-taking; all of these things are laudable, but much more difficult for a disconnected and overworked teacher to note while grading tests and homework. Parents should be aware that many accommodations are allowed through Individual Education Plans (IEPs) that may help ASD students overcome some of these obstacles. Many parents tell me they must specifically ask for such accommodations.

By High School-leaving Age (Age 17–18)…

That brings this discussion to the final year of high school. It is the case that many if not most individuals on the Spectrum have a non-traditional transition to post-school life. I have discovered that while most of the ASD students I work with have the grades and standardized test scores to get into college, not many of them are ready to make that leap. This makes sense, too, considering that college is not just academic, but a completely different way of doing life. It is not just more studying, but more independent living activities and social responsibilities as well. I thought I would list some benchmarks here that would be relatively universal and functional, and not spend too much time trying to identify the different paths an individual could take, and then mapping out the routes.

By school-leaving age, your child should be completely independent when it comes to getting around. This ability can take on many forms. In the US, for example, we really like to drive, and it can be something of a rite of passage to get one's driver's license when turning 16. Due to problems with visual motor skills, anxiety, or other attentional problems, some of our students may choose never to drive. In my experience, of every ten eligible Spectrum drivers (i.e., ASD individuals of appropriate age who can pass the written driver's permit exam), only two or three at most will choose to get their license at the earliest age. This number is likely affected by a number of things, including access to public transportation and parents willing to personally help with transportation.

My guess is that a much larger percentage of these students are capable of driving safely. It was not until working with this population that I met a number of individuals who actively avoided driving. The thought of driving was, for whatever reason, too difficult or aversive for them, and the consequence of not driving was very small (e.g., the child had a parent who would drive them anywhere they wanted to go, and most of the time they did not want to leave the house anyway). The average teenager usually wants a driver's license because of the independence and freedom it represents. If they can then get a car, or use their parents' car, it means more time with friends, more time out of the house and away from parents, and a chance to get a job without having to be embarrassed that your parents are dropping you off. These are a few of the many benefits of a license that do not seem to be tempting to our students. They do not mind being chauffeured by parents, do not have an extensive social life, and are generally happy to be at home (that's where all their stuff is).

Many ASD individuals with a driver's license balk at driving and have to work themselves up to actually get in the car due to anxiety or limited motivation to actually go anywhere. If they cannot or should not drive, what are their options for transportation independence? Public transportation is an option for many who live in or near metropolitan areas. You can find out how skilled they are at getting to and from places on public transportation by actually giving them destinations and activities which require public transportation. If you have not done this, you will likely have to ride with them several times before they can go by themselves. There is also a strong planning component to public transportation—finding bus schedules, timing transfers, figuring out different routes, and so on. There are many online and smartphone applications for getting from Point A to Point B, and these can be invaluable. The key, however, is experience, practice, planning, and repetition. Parents motivated to get their child out of the house will be inventive and creative in making this happen. I have not yet met a motivated parent who is permanently thwarted in this area.

Once your child has a nominal understanding of public transportation or some reliable means of getting around, make it a part of their routine to complete some household chores (even though it might be easier for you to do them yourself). Send them weekly to get eggs from the store, or return/pick up books from the library. Think of that activity which really is out of your way (for me, getting stamps from the post office is a hassle) and make it your child's job. They will argue that it is much more simple and convenient (and thus makes more sense) for you to do this task. You must wade through this "reasoning" (which is largely based on an ego-centric view of the world) and insist. Explain that this is one way your child can contribute to the family and it is a small but important step on the way to becoming an independent adult. Ask them to come up with a better idea on how they can contribute. This should not necessarily have to be a fight. Underneath it all, you likely both want the same thing (a happy child).

By the time of leaving school, your child should be completely independent when it comes to managing a daily schedule. This includes daily activities, such as getting to places on time, going to bed and waking up at the same time; as well as non-standard activities such as making and keeping doctor's appointments. It is my experience that while no life is completely predictable, the vast amount of our days are (or can be) routine. Some people need variety in their day; however, most (if not all) individuals on the Spectrum tend to thrive on routine. Depending on how committed you were to the task, most of your life (75% or more) could become routine. My dogs wake me up at 6am on weekends and know when it is time to eat and go out for a walk. One of my dogs (Pepe) will wake from a dead sleep at 6pm and start barking for his dinner. Your child can get on a routine if Pepe can. Better yet, your child can learn and be successful at establishing and maintaining a routine.

Consequently, there really is no better way to cut oneself off from the community and the outside world than failing to have a routine and schedule. Writers are renowned for utilizing isolation to complete grand literary works, but the ones who live the longest and have the happiest lives are those that talk about their routine. Ray Bradbury was very vocal about his daily routine, treating writing like a job with a start time each day and a minimum word count production. He wrote hundreds of books and lived into his 90s. Your child needs a routine and needs to be personally committed to the routine. I am sure Bradbury, like all of us, got off his routine occasionally, but I would assume he always knew how to get back on and took responsibility for getting himself there.

One of the foundational tasks I have seen that is a huge predictor of future happiness and productivity is the ability to consistently attend, be on time for, and prepared for school. If this is a problem for your child, I think it is wise to make this a priority: no absences or tardies (late to class) for four months, or six months, or a year. You would be surprised at how many other things fall into place when you are on time and ready to go on a consistent basis.

Beyond School

So what is next for your ASD teen? They have a diploma, are off to college or some sort of vocation, military, or volunteer option. Two items determine success at this point and they are the ability to set goals for oneself and the ability to effectively self-advocate.

The list of things that adults normally do with themselves is much, much longer than that for children. The pressure to fit some sort of social, academic, or cultural standard that you and your ASD teen felt when they were in high school is likely diminished somewhat. I can assume, though, that if you are taking the time to read this book, it is likely you do not want your child under-achieving with their future. Modern society places a high premium on the individual contribution. Maybe the answer for your child is not to attend college from the age of 18 to 22 and then get a job in an accounting firm and work there until he or she retires (or maybe it is), but they need to do something. We are happiest when we are busy doing something we find meaningful and fulfilling. I assure you no one finds sleeping 12 hours a day and playing video games 12 hours a day meaningful and fulfilling. It might be fun or relaxing (or safe), but more often than not it is just a way to pass time.

Start with the question of what your child might find meaningful and fulfilling, and think back upon their strengths and interests. For some it is working with animals, for others it is helping with a book drive. From that point, your child should be able to set some goals for getting to the place of doing the activity they find meaningful and fulfilling. They will likely need help in this endeavor. For instance, most of the ASD students I work with say they find designing video games meaningful and fulfilling. They then run into several problems when setting goals. The first is that they set their first goal to "get a job designing video games." The first goal actually needs to be something like "research what kinds of backgrounds your favorite video game designers have" or "get a part-time job at the video game store." Goals should proceed from there.

Second, your adult child should know not only how to self-advocate (ask for help), but how to properly self-advocate (ask for help when needed, in the right way). What is the difference between something you need help with and something you need to persevere and struggle with before you ask for help? When you do ask for help, what are things you can do in your request to make it more likely people will help you? Who is the best person to ask for help? Beyond asking for help, are there things you need to do to avoid being victimized or taken advantage of? Too many ASD teens are passive when they should be actively looking for help, asking questions, or simply moving forward with some sort of action (some sort of motion that helps maintain some momentum). For instance, while they are waiting to hear back from the publishing company they sent their manuscript to for possible publication, they should be avidly reading other books and writing more material.

As a final word in this chapter, adulthood is the time when your child should start reading these books (like the one you are reading) and seeking out therapy for themselves. There are an ever-increasing number of self-help books specifically for the adult on the Spectrum. Tell them to get to work.

PART II

GROWTH AND DEVELOPMENT

CHAPTER 5

WHAT HAPPENS WHEN A CHILD BECOMES AN ADOLESCENT (WHO IS BIGGER THAN YOU)?

Some developmental delays in Autism Spectrum Disorder (ASD) children, and especially children diagnosed with Asperger Syndrome (AS) and Non-verbal Learning Disorder (NLD), seem to become more pronounced as the child ages. This may have something to do with the increasing discrepancy between the child's physical size (which usually proceeds developmentally at a typical pace) and their behavior (developmentally delayed). Simple interventions I have made have been helping ASD teens modify their vocabulary, or look for a more age-appropriate version of the thing in which they are interested.

Working on this issue is important on two levels. First, the more age-appropriate and the more conforming to society's rules you are, the better treatment you will get. I am not making this statement as a way to say I think it is fair, it is simply the reality of living in a society. Second, if you actively break rules and defy what people expect of you, and you do it in a way people see as threatening, things will get much worse for you, and really quickly. Let us talk about attracting good attention first.

Getting What You Want

I like talking with my students about language. It is an area of interest of mine, and of most ASD individuals I have met. I also really appreciate the vocabulary skills of my ASD students. One thing I have encouraged students to examine is the meaning and connotation of the word "toy" as a pragmatic language activity. An adolescent I was working with would use a phrase like "I was playing with my toys…" when I asked him to tell me something about his week. The phrase sounded strange coming out of the mouth of this near adult-sized young man, so I asked him to tell me specifically what he was doing when playing. What he described was building a scale model of the item he was interested in (he was surprisingly dexterous). After explaining to him how he sounded when he said he was playing with toys, and what people might think of him when they heard him say this, we decided to practice using the phrase "model building." I had him use this as part of his response for several weeks when I asked him what was new. We also continued to talk about the meaning of certain words, and how certain words were reserved for certain individuals or groups. After a while of struggling with the meaning and connotation of the word "toy" (he did not understand how use of the word was typically reserved for young children, or in reference to young children's playthings), he decided to train himself to stop using the word altogether. I thought this was an appropriate compromise.

Words and word use are important when interacting with others. We want people to be relatively accurate when making guesses and assumptions about us when we interact with them. For instance, we want people to make relatively accurate guesses about our intellect, age, openness, agreeableness, and friendliness. Assumptions about these qualities, and many more, are all a part of the first impression. How we present ourselves to others in these quick bursts of information (usually non-verbal) can be the difference between getting what we want from the person (e.g., accurate directions to the nearest bathroom) or not. It is important to teach ASD teens that their actions (e.g., their pragmatic language use, how they say what they say) and their appearance (e.g., grooming, clothing, facial expressions) give others a lot of information about you. Especially important is when one's behaviors give a false and negative impression, or the impression that you are dangerous or a threat.

Being Seen as a Threat

ASD teens that throw tantrums, or become overly exuberant, loud, or make large, full-body motions in public when they get upset will be looked at as, at best, someone to avoid. I come right out and say to my students who do these behaviors, "You look like you are crazy. Is that how you are intending to look?" They always reply that it is not their intent to look crazy, so I recommend to them to stop doing that particular behavior. At worst, these children could have been deemed to be a threat. Modern society responds to such physical threats in a way contrary to what ASD teens who are upset enough to throw a fit actually need. Usually, people who are responding to the perceived threat (e.g., security personnel) succeed at escalating the situation with ASD teens. The security personnel can ask questions, make demands and ultimatums, and sometimes have the authority to get physically involved in the act of reducing the perceived threat. Most ASD teens do not do well with security personnel, and especially when they are upset. It almost always gets worse.

If you have an ASD teen who tends to get more boisterous, louder, or more physically active when they are upset, I would highly recommend this as something you work on with your child. In this space I cannot go into any specific interventions because this is something about which you should be consulting a therapist or other professional. I will give you some of my parameters when dealing with this issue, though, in hopes that they give you some guidelines and help you make some decisions.

The easiest way to get a child who is physically out of control to stop hitting and throwing things is to physically subdue them (I am not recommending this intervention, or any form of it). Parents throughout history have found that applying gentle pressure through a hug-like hold can be one of the most effective and efficient ways to help a child regain composure and calm down (after an initial burst of energy from the person being subdued). Consequently, big brothers all over the world are aware of this maneuver for getting little brothers to do their bidding. The hug-like hold is so effective, though, that some parents use it exclusively as a method to calm their children down. When young children who have tantrums become adolescents who have tantrums is usually the time when parents seek out my services. Usually the parent tells me they are worried about the child hurting someone in the midst of a fit or tantrum, especially those who try to get close to the child to calm them.

Minimum Height Requirement

Different families have different methods of parenting, but parents and professionals alike have discovered that creatively rewarding positive behaviors (on a randomized schedule) is effective in getting the behaviors from your child that you want, almost all the time. Some parents feel, however, that their child can get too worked up or upset to listen to reason or be able to process alternatives to having a tantrum or throwing a fit. So, for these parents who choose to physically subdue their children when their child is upset and a threat to themselves or someone else, my number one rule for physical confrontations in the house is that once the child has grown to your height or taller, you should no longer allow or expect physical contact when the child is upset, or as a way of motivating or forcing your child to do something. If your child is as tall or taller than any adult in the house (Mom or Dad), under no circumstances should either Mom or Dad become physical with them when they are upset.

What does one do in these circumstances then? If your child is not in therapy at this point, see this as a sign to get them in right away. Do not delay this action. Children who are physically out of control are disruptive to the very foundation of the family's daily functioning. You have been living with the anticipation of this physical altercation so long you likely do not realize just how disruptive this has been to your family.

Therapy is beneficial for a long-term fix, but what does one do in the meantime? You cannot and should not physically interact with your out-of-control child, but someone can. I have encouraged parents to make a call to the proper authorities. Some cities and municipalities in the US, for example, are fortunate enough to have a service called a Mobile Crisis Unit (MCU). MCUs are trained health care and mental health care professionals who are on call 24 hours a day and will drive out to wherever you are to help you defuse a crisis situation (broadly defined). Unfortunately, when municipalities fall on hard times, MCU services and those like them are discontinued. You might need to call the police or local law enforcement authorities to intervene instead.

Nearly every parent I talk to about calling the police on their child has at least minor reservations about this action. They are worried that their child will be arrested, taken into custody, placed in child protective services, or separated from the family. Other parents worry that the police officer might blame the parent for the child's behavior and criticize or arrest them. Some parents worry that calling the police will make the out-of-control child's behavior escalate, will embarrass them in front of the neighbors, cause the child to feel betrayed, and permanently damage the relationship. All of these concerns make sense to me, and based on the extraordinary examples of police interaction we hear from the news media or entertainment media, I do not think these concerns are unfounded.

Despite these concerns, I will tell you that every parent I have worked with who has made this choice to call the police on their out-of-control child reports to me that they found themselves legitimately concerned about the safety of their child or someone in the house (including the parent who made the telephone call), and saw that action as a turning point in the functioning of the household. The child is always surprised when the parent calls the police and the police show up. Finally, if the parent made it clear to the child, prior to the incident that precipitated the call to the police, exactly what behaviors (e.g., threats of safety to self or others) would inspire a call to the police, the child always walks away from the encounter with the police with some understanding and context for how his or her behavior led to the call. In a sense, the parents report to me, they eventually feel exonerated by their children.

Who is Serving Whom?

I ask the above header question in many forms to parents who find themselves out of options in maintaining peace in their households. Who is in charge? Who makes the final decisions? Whose responsibility is it to provide for the safety and stability of the house? Are parents supposed to be subject to the whims (or even needs) of their children? Most modern societies set the bar for providing basic needs to children at food, shelter, safety, and education. This is the minimum that society expects you to provide your child. Most people would set the minimum bar a little higher and state that children also need unconditional love and acceptance. I think these are good additions to the list.

Beyond that, it is all up for negotiation. Crafty and savvy parents can use the rest of the seeming necessities (mobile phones, computers, free time, pizza for dinner, etc.) as incentives for behavior that leads to a smoothly running household. Children are not required to have a mobile phone. They do not need to have time to play video games each day, but they can certainly earn it. Children must actively contribute to a smoothly running household, and too many parents get caught up in the incorrect assumptions of the child that these extras are, in fact, rights, or something they deserve as a function of being alive. I encourage all parents to have the discussion about rights versus privileges with their ASD teens to make sure everyone is on the same page.

An example layout of a bedroom that contains only the things society insists parents provide children includes (*note:* all must be clean):

- mattress (bed frame optional)
- sheets
- blanket
- pillow
- a lamp
- enough age-appropriate clothing to maintain proper hygiene
- some place to put clothing (closet, dresser)
- alarm clock (not a right, but a good idea).

Things children have in their bedroom they feel they need, but do not in fact need, include:

- computer
- video game console
- telephone or mobile phone
- TV
- toys, books, magazines
- food (this can stay in the shared eating area)
- desk and chair
- piles of clothing
- posters on the wall
- multiples of items listed above.

In addition to physical objects, teens sometimes feel they deserve certain intangible items. My favorite intangible item to discuss with children is "free time." Children do not automatically deserve free time. The family may benefit from the child having free time, but most parents will note that children do not inherently know how to properly manage it. It is not uncommon for me to hear arguments between parents and children in my office about the use of free time. Many ASD teens argue that they cannot or will not do things such as chores, homework, or spend time with the family (all are legitimate duties of teens) because it cuts in on their free time. To my continued astonishment, parents continue to legitimize that argument. "Yes," they say, "Kyle needs his free time. We will find some other way to get the trash taken out."

That children may benefit from parent-directed free time, or a desk, chair, and computer in their room, is true. That they deserve free time, or inherently know how to use free time, or deserve any other items from the second list, is false. By believing otherwise you are relinquishing your best items for negotiation and motivation.

Apple and Tree

Over the years psychologists and other mental health professionals have struggled to describe the origins of the Spectrum disabilities accurately. Rather than shedding light on a perplexing quandary, we have mostly succeeded in blaming and alienating parents in their pursuits to do right by their children. For example, an early cause of Autism that was suggested by the professional community was that the autistic child's mother was cold and uncaring. We now laugh that such a false and ridiculous theory could ever have been taken seriously, but it was, by many heartbroken parents. I am not surprised when I meet parents who clearly feel like there was something they could have done to spare their child from having AS, or NLD, or any of the other neurocognitive disorders discussed in this book. Parents tell me they feel they could have spared their child years or frustration, struggle, agony, and suffering if they had done some part of the parenting process differently.

This type of thinking usually expresses itself in two main ways: guilt and anger/contempt. Both ways of looking at your child's diagnosis make effective parenting nearly impossible. Both responses also can have a profoundly negative impact on your child.

Guilt

Some parents falsely believe that there is something they could have done differently to save their child from having a life of struggle. The first thing I say to that is there is nothing you or anyone could have done to save your child from a life of struggle. I know this because (a) there is no inoculation or intervention available to prevent these syndromes, and (b) life is a struggle for everyone (not just people on the Spectrum). No parent can tell me that they had an easy life. All good parents have had challenge in their lives, and the expectation should always have been to learn and grow stronger from challenge, not avoid it. Growing stronger from challenge builds character, which is what makes people want to be around us. Most of the ASD teens I know abound in character and are easy to appreciate and like. I think this surplus of character is often related to their surplus of struggle.

Parents who feel guilty about their ASD child's life and diagnosis seem more likely to make unhelpful compromises for their children. They seem more likely to remove obstacles for their children, eliminate struggles, and artificially lower demands and expectations. In addition to lowering demands, they seem to lower their standards for their child's behavior and achievements. In practical terms, they may look for small, petty things to point to when praising their child. They might also find themselves making excuses for their child's behavior, or intervening when intervention is not necessary. What started off as an effort to protect the ego and build self-esteem turns out to build contempt in both the child and the parent. Children can also be confused about what the world expects of them or continue the tradition of setting artificially low standards for themselves.

Anger/Contempt

Some parents I talk to speak as if their child is intentionally disabled, or performing behaviors consistent with a Spectrum diagnosis on purpose. A classic example is the ASD individual who has trouble falling asleep at night (common to individuals on the Spectrum) and, thus, problems waking up in the morning. Angry parents are likely to suggest that the child is lazy, or entitled, and that they were up at 6am, even on weekends, as a teenager. They express exasperation at the behavior of their children and often offer advice or direction to their children that includes general statements like, "Pull yourself together," "Suck it up," "I never did that when I was your age," and other unhelpful encouragements. I meet parents who overtly express anger at their children verbally through cutting or degrading remarks, critically compare the child to a sibling, or even withdraw from active parenting all together. When I interview these parents, they invariably suggest that some of their child's disabilities are due to laziness, lack of effort or caring, or an intentional effort to make the parent angry.

I can only imagine the path that brings these parents to the point of disliking or being angry at their child for behaviors or characteristics that are expressions of their disability. Some parents do not believe that AS or NLD are real things. They look at the struggles their children have and conclude they are not trying hard enough. I think some parents start out feeling guilty about their child's life and then adopt a more self-centered approach to the problem and blame their child for failing to live up to expectations.

I think other parents are embarrassed at the behavior of their child, and are jealous of the stories they hear of the children of friends who are achieving things their child cannot or will not (or has no interest in). Guilt, disappointment, blame, discontent: all these attitudes germinate contempt and bitterness. The reality, though, is that children know when their parents do not like them and are disappointed by their behavior or lack of accomplishment. They sense the unreasonable hurdle to affection and acceptance that is being placed in front of them, and this allows the seed of self-contempt to germinate and grow.

What is a Parent to Do?

The line between expectations that are high and those that are unreasonable is challenging to negotiate. It requires a continually updated understanding of the abilities and needs of the child. Having a trusted professional help you discover, define, and walk that line can be invaluable. Simply having someone to talk to (it can be another parent) that does not live in the house with you and your ASD teen can be a huge help. I think the process of setting and updating expectations for your ASD teen is going to be constant, but persistence in this case will pay off. Some guidelines in your process:

- Be honest.

- Be clear.

- Be creative.

- Be studious.

- Be flexible.

- Focus on the fundamentals:

    ◦ rights vs. privileges

    ◦ creating happy, productive adults

    ◦ authoritative parenting (high warmth/high expectations; Baumrind 1966)

    ◦ routine and predictability.

- Get help when needed.

- Be safe.

Consequently, if you do not have a reliable partner in parenting, I would highly recommend that you locate and begin fostering a relationship with another parent who can be a support to you. More and more parents that I work with these days are joining parent support groups. If you have not been to one, I think it is worth checking out. Wait to decide what is and is not for you after you have tried it.

Acceptance

In the same way that most ASD children I meet go through the process of accepting the realities of their diagnosis, parents must learn to accept the reality that their child is on the Spectrum. I will encourage all parents, regardless how caring and compassionate you seem to be, to recognize that this will be a process that will take time. This process will also take you beyond feeling sorry for your child and will lead you to having realistic expectations for how your child is going to contribute uniquely to society. Participating in this process is essential to effective parenting, so I encourage you to make it a priority. For some parents the first step is to let go of the notion that your child will be cured of their disorder. For others it can be letting go of the notion that your child will attend your alma mater, or have a passion for playing sports like you did. Still others simply need to find some way to connect with their child. Keep looking, keep searching. Accepting and connecting with your child is an endeavor worth pursuing.

CHAPTER 6

RULES, JUSTICE, AND THE SEARCH FOR PEACE

This chapter will explain to parents or other interested parties just what motivates and inspires the interpersonal behaviors of Autism Spectrum Disorder (ASD) individuals. Of course this cannot be a description of all motivations of all ASD individuals in all situations. What I want to bring up are some overarching themes I have discovered in my time working with ASD individuals.

Interpersonal Social Behavior

People remark that ASD individuals can be unpredictable in their socializing and social interactions. I find the students I work with have a unique perspective on life, including beliefs about how the world works and why it works that way. ASD individuals are described as outside-the-box thinkers, and I believe that is because, when one is not aware of much social convention, one is not necessarily restricted by it. Most of us have to work to think outside the box and be creative. ASD individuals were either never in the box to begin with or not aware that there is a box, so thinking outside the box is simply just "thinking."

I can see at least two types of interpersonal social behavior in common society. The first is what I will call scripted social behavior. These are behaviors you perform when you are cued or you can anticipate the interaction. For instance, most people have a script for eating at a restaurant, or talking to a school principal, or attending a wedding. We know how to behave in these situations even though we do not know most of the specifics of the situation (e.g., who will be there, what the conversation will be about, who is in the wedding party). Most of us learn most of these scripted behaviors by having numerous interpersonal interactions and experiences and learning from mistakes (called social faux pas).

We actually learn very few scripted behaviors from direct instruction, relative to all the behaviors we master. Because ASD individuals struggle with non-verbal communication, they do not normally learn much scripted social behavior in this way (e.g., through the perpetual feedback loop we get from our mother's glare when we are too loud at the wedding). Most ASD students I know learn about scripted behaviors in social skills class or through some other type of direct instruction and intentional practice such as role-play activities. A good example of scripted social behavior is how one acts and what one does at a birthday party. Most people know that you bring a gift (unless you are told not to, and then sometimes you do anyway), you eat cake, you make small-talk with people you may not know or may not see often, you sing a particular song, and on and on. The point is that there is a way one should act at birthday parties, and we all pretty much know what that is without reading a "how to attend a birthday party and be socially successful there" style book. ASD individuals need the instructions to achieve the same level of competency that Neurotypicals (NTs) seem to pick up without too much effort.

The second type of social interaction is what I will call spontaneous social interaction. An example of this is seeing someone on the subway you went to school with, and have not seen in a number of years. Another is when two people reach for the last donut. Finally, people can ask questions or pose topics in discussions ("What do you think about America's foreign involvement in nation-building?") that are unanticipated or jarring, and a spontaneous social interaction for which there is limited script can ensue. These situations are not very typical, and so most people do not have a lot of experience with them. Most people do not have a script for what to do when you see a long-lost school friend on the subway, and they have to guess how to act. In most cases it is left to chance whether the interaction is going to be gratifying or awkward.

The reality is that the fewer social scripts you know, the more spontaneous social interactions you are likely to have. It is in these spontaneous interactions that the most bizarre or unexpected behavior can come out for all people. Parents report being embarrassed at the behavior of their children, surprised, angered, upset, offended, amazed, blown away, or blindsided. To the casual observer, the behavior of ASD individuals can be fantastic, peculiar, hilarious, or creative. Not surprisingly I spend a significant amount of my time trying to guess what ASD individuals are thinking, and then interpreting what I find out to parents or other interested parties. The point of this section is that regardless of how the behavior of ASD individuals looks in these spontaneous social interactions, their behavior is not random. All behavior is inspired and flows from one or several basic life principles. My hope is that by uncovering some of these basic life principles you will be able to understand the behavior of your ASD teen better. Good parenting is founded upon understanding and compassion.

Anticipation of Motivation

There is incredible value in knowing what motivates your ASD child. Because the perspectives of parents and their ASD children are often so disparate, this can be both a fascinating and frustrating journey for parents. But when one knows what inspires the behavior, one can make predictions about future behaviors. Being able to guess what your child is thinking and might do next is good for lots of reasons.

Knowing what inspires behavior allows us to anticipate questions, gaps in knowledge, and problems. This means that you can guess what situations might be already scripted for your child (and not require much prep work) and what might be spontaneous (and require prep work). One of my favorite recent stories was from a couple who were preparing their child to attend a funeral. They put their heads together to anticipate all of the areas their child might struggle with or have questions about during the ceremony. They went through and discussed the entire event with their child, and came up with contingencies for unanticipated events. They practiced and practiced because funerals are particularly bad places to make social faux pas. When the funeral was over and the bereaved had exited the place of worship, the parents could tell that their child was bursting with a question. They went with one of their contingency plans and told the child to wait two minutes for them to get to the car. When the family was buckled in and completely free of any chance of embarrassment from onlookers, they cued the child to ask his question. "What was in the box?" the child asked.

Understanding of motivation also allows us to identify with our children. Identification usually leads to empathy, and empathic responding. It is my greatest pleasure to talk with frustrated parents about why their child is doing something frustrating or embarrassing. I do this a lot with children who are misbehaving and pushing limits in the house. I tell the parents that pushing limits is the job of the teen and it is developmentally appropriate. It is the way that all of us learn about cause and effect in the social realm, rules, limits, consequences, and all the other things we need to learn in order to be socially successful. When I tell parents that there is a purpose to the misbehavior, and it certainly is not for the purpose of ruining the parents' day, parents can relax. They understand the motivation of behavior, can identify with the child's experience, and often increase in empathic (and constructive) responding to their child.

Parents who also understand the motivation of their children often find more commonalities with their children, and more places to identify and bond with them. This can be especially important for parents of ASD children who report to me that they struggle to find things in common with their child. Relationships between parents and children can strengthen through understanding of motivation.

Finally, finding the underlying driving force behind any type of action (but especially social) gives parents a better understanding of the strengths, weaknesses, and preferences of their children. This is invaluable when you begin the discussion about higher education and vocation. My current career is not a typical one, but I knew it when I saw it because my parents had, for most of my life, talked with me about what I was good at, what I was bad at, and what things I seemed to prefer. Rather than feeling boxed in, it is my experience that children who have these kinds of discussions with knowledgeable and insightful parents seem to be more self-confident, self-assured, and self-directed.

Rules as Foundation of Order

In my discussions with ASD individuals, I have found an underlying theme to how many of them approach the world. Many individuals with ASD seem to find the world mysterious and scary, and many see parts of the world (especially many social parts) as unknowable. Those children who spent more time in the wrong academic setting seem to have a more unshakeable view of the world as scary and unknowable. We know this from the literature on learned helplessness (Seligman and Maier 1967; Seligman 1972). People who try, and fail over and over, eventually stop trying, even when the solution is pointed out to them.

Without reliable access to the non-verbal information that much of us have about the world, there is a lot left to the imagination. It is for this reason, I believe, that ASD individuals place a high value on concrete rules. This is especially the case for social interactions. My students value and listen most intently to the statements that start with "Every time…" Every time you see someone for the first time in the day, say hello. Every time someone holds their hand out to shake, grasp it with a firm grip and shake it back, with one pump only. Every time someone gives you something (even verbal information), say thank you.

Rules help create predictable situations and allow more accuracy when forecasting and planning. The more you can anticipate, the more you can rely on scripts, the less you have to engage in spontaneous social interactions, the fewer mistakes you are likely to make, the less embarrassed you will be, and on and on. Rules can help reduce anxiety and can lead to an overall increase in comfort and enjoyment. The problem with social interactions is that there are very few concrete rules. Modern society, and especially modern teen society, is in a constant state of change and upheaval. Rigidly applying outdated or discrete rules can look just as strange as having no rule to apply in the first place. Regardless, rules allow us a place to start, a foundation for order.

When specific rules (e.g., in X situation, perform Y behavior) do not apply, one can move to the level of applying concepts. Concepts can give one a clue to the category of behavior expected. Concepts such as fairness, justice, and equality seem particularly attractive to ASD individuals. Perhaps that attraction comes from the fact that these concepts are highly universal. Fairness, justice, and equality are concepts that are discussed and addressed across all media, and throughout history.

It could also be the case that these concepts can logically lead to the restoration of peace and balance. When someone wrongs someone else, fairness dictates that the exact same behavior can be done back to them, and that will cause things to become balanced again. The physics of relationships and interpersonal interactions dictates that this approach never works, but the elegant simplicity of the "eye for an eye" exchange can be enticing.

How Perspective-taking Plays a Role

You may hear your ASD teen use phrases such as "That isn't fair" long past when it seems developmentally appropriate. They seem, when saying this, to truly not understand how an event played out. They can become especially annoyed when it seems like everyone else is okay with an event that they see as unfair. I typically expect to hear "That isn't fair" from a child up to about 13 years of age. When a child reaches adolescence, they begin to develop a more complex view of how the world works, and they start to let go of the notion that fairness rules exchanges. Also, children tend to get the idea (because their parent has said it for the thousandth time) that they should not expect life to be fair all the time, and they do, in fact, have a very comfortable life. Seeing your experience in relation to that of others is not an activity that comes naturally to the ASD individual. Fairness and justice concepts can be over-applied and misapplied. It is my experience, though, that a deeper understanding of fairness and justice can be acquired as the ASD child becomes an adult.

A common social misapplication of the justice and fairness concept I have seen is when ASD children talk to adults in the same way that they talk to their peers. Most people know that one must differentiate between people higher and lower on the social hierarchy through formality of language. Children should use more proper phrases like "please" and "thank you" with adults than they do with peers. Children typically also use less slang with adults, and we do not correct the behavior of those above us in the hierarchy at any time (even when they ask us to). ASD individuals can get into a lot of trouble socially for an over-application of fairness across the social hierarchy. On the one hand, it makes sense and actually seems ideal that everybody gets treated the same. On the other hand, modern society, no matter how progressive, depends on differentiation of individuals based on their place in the hierarchy of social order. We do that by treating people differently based on their place in the hierarchy.

At this point it should be noted that some families I work with do not recognize or practice hierarchy in their homes (e.g., parents expecting children to display a minimum amount of respect for their position as provider and heads of family), or are much more relaxed about it. I want to note that most workplace cultures and businesses apply very strict interpretations of hierarchy. Teaching your child to recognize hierarchy and respond appropriately to it eliminates one more hurdle to gainful employment and independent living. It is also hard to fault someone for being too respectful and polite.

I have had some success getting past the difficulty understanding social hierarchy by helping my students create some concrete rules for interacting with others up, down, and across the social hierarchy. They include:

- Always be polite, no matter what.

- Use furniture only for its designated purpose (and definitely no feet on furniture, including seats on public transportation).

- Always say hello when someone greets you.

- Do not walk away from people while they are talking to you.

- Never argue with a police officer.

- Immediately call your parents when you do not know what to do.

Most people can generate a few rules that will work (or at least not make things worse) in most situations. Parents have had wonderful success teaching their children to say thank you whenever an adult gives them something. Most people appreciate, and certainly no one can fault, good manners.

Perspective-taking allows us to anticipate what someone expects from us. We can take on someone's role and see the situation through their eyes. This ability, I have found, becomes more adaptive as a person ages. The reality of life, and especially the work world, is that specificity of expectations and rules for action tend to decrease as the person gets older and has more responsibility. Your boss tells you she wants you to solve a personnel issue, or hire a contractor for the renovation, but beyond those general expectations you are also expected to figure out the specific course of action. If you struggle to see things from the perspective of others (empathy), you are going to struggle with fulfilling expectations.

I do believe ASD individuals are highly empathic, but struggle with both interpreting correctly that empathic information, and letting others know that they have access to the empathic information. Some ASD individuals I have talked to have doggedly practiced empathic interpretation and, through trial and error and checking in with people they can trust, can get very good at empathic understanding of specific individuals. Others have learned how to ask questions effectively to discern the expectations of others. The key in this case is to ask just the right amount of questions. You want your target to feel good about your level of understanding of expectations, but not feel like they are doing all the work for you. Also, bosses usually have their own work to do and need to be able to rely on their workers to make good guesses about what is expected of them.

The question often comes up as to what the process is in shifting from following scripts in social situations to being able to improvise or respond fluidly to novel social situations. There are two points to be made here. First, some have suggested (Rourke 1995) that inability to respond fluidly and spontaneously in social situations is part of the disorder. It is possible that attempting to achieve fluidity and spontaneity in social situations is not a good use of time for the ASD individual. Second, most of daily living is composed of patterned, scripted events. For those that like predictability and a sense of social mastery, scripted events can be sought out through creating routines. My hope for ASD individuals, however, is that they can learn to see these unscripted events as less stressful and catastrophic than they might. The reality is that everyone, at some time, finds themselves in awkward social situations and is embarrassed about how they have responded. We all endeavor to limit these situations and do better the next time. I encourage all ASD individuals to reflect on and process their social interactions. If you feel your interaction was less than ideal, get some advice about how to do it differently next time.

Experience

As we age, we shift from fluid intelligence to crystallized intelligence for help in making decisions. Fluid intelligence is finesse and problem-solving. Crystallized intelligence is based much more on prior knowledge and experience for generating solutions to problems. One of the things I have noticed about some of the ASD teens I work with is that they can flat-out reject the notion that I might know the answer to a question or problem based solely on my experience. This is as opposed to Neurotypical (NT) teens who will at least concede that I might be right, but are still committed to doing it their own way. ASD teens will say that I cannot possibly be right because they have pursued a line of logic and have come to a different conclusion. ASD teens seem to struggle with properly valuing experience, or understanding that someone else could have experienced the same thing and come to a different conclusion.

This is an especially difficult way of thinking to overcome, because it is something that you do not know that you do not know. You have no context for knowing, so how could you be aware that you are unaware? Many ASD teens dismiss the liability of ignorance in the same way that they dismiss the value of experience.

Added to this, many ASD teens do not spontaneously reflect on their experience. I have had more than one ASD student refuse to discuss a past situation with me. They state their refusal in almost the same way each time: "It is over, it is in the past, there is no reason to talk about it any more." Try as I might, I cannot convince them of the value of reflection for learning. Mistakes allow some of the most fertile ground for reflection and learning, and one handicaps oneself by refusing to engage in the process.

Sometimes I can convince a student to reflect and deconstruct the experience, but I have also noticed that there is very little spontaneity to the reflective process. By this I mean that this student would not have reflected on the experience (regardless of the quality of the experience) if I had not cued him to do so. Teens in general are very much "now-oriented," but I do believe the Spectrum disorder amplifies this orientation and makes it harder to focus outside of the now. I have joked that ASD individuals would find much of Zen Buddhism as second-nature because of the focus on being in the "here and now" and focusing exclusively on the present experience. Meditation and Mindfulness also use these strategies, and I do believe ASD individuals find these activities more natural to their state of being than the general population. But getting an ASD individual to intentionally go back to a past experience and process it can be a challenge. Interestingly, this can span from reflecting on a problematic social interaction to checking answers on an exam paper before handing it in.

So, what happens when your tendency is to ignore or devalue the role of experience, or when you do not spontaneously reflect on your own experience so as to gain useful information? Many of my students engage in a false logic. Their thinking might be orderly and methodical, but if any of their assumptions are incorrect, their conclusion is flawed. When conclusions are incorrect, resulting actions can look strange or mysterious.

What is the solution? I make a big deal out of it when I am right and they are wrong. This does, of course, lead to some resentment, but one of the benefits of living in the now is the ability to let go of that resentment pretty easily. I also make it a point to make predictions about a lot of stuff they are not asking me about. You might be surprised, if you start doing this, just how much of life is predictable and orderly. By your making predictions and being right a lot, ASD teens can begin to place a value on your correctness. You can then explain to them that you have access to this information through a process of reflection, and the accumulation of experience, and that they can have access to the same information if they would engage in that process as well.

Teachers I have worked with who teach the process of reflection to ASD teens tell me it can be laborious. If a parent would like to help their ASD child with building or refining reflective abilities, I would suggest basing the process on their child's strength. Is your

ASD child good at verbal interactions, or writing things down, or creating graphic depictions of things (pictures)? Use those media for the process. Then come up with a set of questions that will cue the process, such as, "What did you like about this experience?", "What worked for you?", "What advice would you give someone who is doing this for the first time?" I try to focus on the positive because many ASD teens I know reflect on the negative or catastrophic without prompting and have a hard time moving away from that. Then, you should give your child some examples of appropriate or useful responses to each of the questions. After that, it's practice, practice, practice. The process should become somewhat automatic but will still require prompting with time.

Efforts for Peace and Balance

Most ASD teens I talk to express some level of frustration at not being able to discern the expectations of others. This seems to lead to a frustration loop. They are given instructions that they are frustrated to discover they do not understand fully. The giver of the instructions is now frustrated that the ASD teen does not fully understand and is clearly frustrated, which leads to more and more frustration, and usually a premature and unsatisfying termination of the interaction.

What the ASD teen wanted in the first place, more than anything else, was to maintain balance with their environment. The expectations of adults are usually seen as threatening this balance. They want to be in balance with their physical environment in that they want to be physically comfortable. They want a balance with their internal environment and want to be able to control their mood and anxiety. They also want a balance with their social environment. Not all ASD teens need copious amounts of praise and affection, but they certainly do not want people being upset with them or disappointed with them.

I want to be clear that most ASD teens I talk to are aware, at various levels, that they have failed to meet the expectations of others. This is important to know because the response of the average teen, and especially an ASD teen, can be one of lack of awareness or concern for the feelings of others. This response can be upsetting to the onlooker, and especially the adult who is trying to teach the child to be a good person. In cases like these I have no problem teaching ASD children to perform the pragmatic language skills of someone who cares, regardless of how they feel about the situation. I can do this because I know that at the heart of most ASD teens, they are committed to peace and balance just like me.

Finally, the following is based exclusively on what I have observed over the last number of years working with the ASD population. ASD teens are not necessarily looking for good-will among men, so to speak. They seem to be less interested in everybody liking them and more interested in the absence of ill-will. I get the sense that most of my ASD students really do not care what I think of them inasmuch as none of them are showing me their work and looking for praise. They really care, however, if I criticize them and make them change. But again, I think they are only interested in my approval so long as it means I will generally leave them alone and let them do their thing. This is quite possibly one of the greatest and most fascinating differences between the NT population and the ASD population. When creating a sense of self, the average ASD teen seems to be able to completely ignore the opinions of authorities like me.

CHAPTER 7

MORALITY AND BEING A GOOD PERSON

Discussing morality is a challenge, especially in modern society. At the outset, I want to say that I fully trust the Native Expert (you, the parent) to be capable of teaching your children to be moral individuals. With that said, sometimes people could use some help on how to do that, and especially in an area that requires the moral individual to focus intensely on others. I also realize that morality and goodness are not always synonymous. All of these discussions (e.g., what is morality, what is goodness, how does it all relate to modern society?) are certainly outside the realm of this book. I think we can all agree, however, that it would be nice if society saw our children as good people, and if our children knew how to make decisions based on moral principles. Goodness and morality are pretty universal, and most religions, cultures, and ideologies cannot fault people for trying (or looking like they are trying) to be good. When prioritizing social skills training for Autism Spectrum Disorder (ASD) teens, we should look for the behaviors that will make the largest positive impact.

Theory of Mind (TOM) plays a strong part in moral reasoning and the appearance of being good. After all, if you want people to think you are a good person, you need to know what they think good people do. The very first step in this whole process, for ASD children, is realizing that other people constantly make judgments about us based on our behavior. Second, people have some pretty specific expectations for our behavior, and these expectations are usually formalized in the sense that most people know what they are without having to talk about them and compare notes much. These expectations can take the obvious form of laws (e.g., it is unlawful to assault another person), but often when speaking about morals they are implicit social norms.

TOM, at its core, is the ability to recognize that others have minds (and, thus, experiences, opinions, beliefs, etc.) that are different from our own. It is a cognitive (thinking) activity, and a skill that is developmentally based. Little children have very limited TOM skills, but get better at it as they mature. This increase in skill is a function of both development of different parts of the brain (specifically, the prefrontal cortex) and practice. When you hear a parent saying to a child, "How would you like it if I did something like that to you?", the parent is inadvertently helping the child practice TOM. Empathy is related to TOM (perhaps it is a technique that helps us develop or refine TOM) where we try to imagine the actual experience of others for the purpose of knowing how to interact with them. Empathic responding is a valuable trait in modern society because it usually leads to the most effective forms of care-taking. Empathy is not just recognition of affective (emotional) states, but physical states as well.

TOM and empathy have been hotly debated recently in terms of Spectrum disorders. It is traditionally the argument that individuals on the Spectrum suffer from under-developed or even absent abilities in TOM, and thus a limited ability to empathize. This creates a whole range of problems because empathy is a desirable commodity in modern society. Recently, I have been intrigued by the evolution of this debate in professional circles. My own experience tells me that individuals on the Spectrum experience empathy at least as much as Neurotypicals (NTs). In fact, I know many ASD individuals who seem to be less guarded against taking on the experiences of others than the average individual.

The difference, I have noted, is in two areas. First, most ASD individuals seem not to know what to do with the empathic information they receive. They seem to have trouble discerning its source in the environment it is coming from (a TOM activity), and then what to do with it. Most people can identify an empathic response they are having, and then manage it (e.g., separate themselves from the source, talk themselves through their response). For instance, when a person watches a sad movie, it is not uncommon for them to be sad as a result. When you ask them why they are sad, they will likely tell you that they just watched a sad movie. In this same scenario, when you ask the ASD individual why they are sad, they might not be able to identify the movie as the source of sadness, or might point to an unrelated experience.

Second, empathy and empathic responding require a good deal of pragmatic language. One must initially read a lot of non-verbal cues in order to understand and make sense of the experience of another person, then one must let others know that they understand. This is called using receptive (taking information in) language and expressive (reporting out) language skills. Expressive and receptive language use is a weakness in most ASD individuals. So, even if the ASD individual is having an empathic experience, and can interpret their experience in a productive way, letting you know that they know can be a challenging activity. This is all to say that raising a good, moral person (the job of the Native Expert) is a great place to start, but the difficult task for ASD individuals is mastering the behaviors that society attributes to good, moral people.

I Didn't Realize You Had Needs

A common complaint I hear from parents is that their ASD child seems to be completely unaware of the needs of other people. Usually, by this, the parent means the child never helps out around the house, rarely says "thank you," might not buy a Father's Day gift without extensive prompting from Mom, or things like that.

For the record, teenagers in general are relatively self-centered. This is a developmentally appropriate state of being for teenagers. Without training, most people remain self-centered as well, and usually until they have children of their own they are committed to raising. Most parents need to adjust their expectations when it comes to the selflessness of their children. Teens need direct instruction on thinking about others.

ASD individuals, however, seem to need to work extra hard at recognizing the experience of others and responding in an effective way. What many parents are seeing as intentional self-centeredness ("You don't care about anyone but yourself!") is actually a developmental delay. In most of these situations, the oversight is truly unintentional. It did not even occur to the ASD individual that someone else had a need, let alone what the need was at the time they were having it. Or that the expectation was that they would notice the need. Or that they should respond in a way that helped fulfill the need. Or that they were even able to respond in a way that helped fulfill the need. In the same way, most ASD individuals I work with are unaware that the fulfilling of their own needs requires work from other people. Some people seem to keep this big ledger in their minds about what they owe, and what they are owed. We are reluctant to borrow someone's car because we know we will have to fill it with fuel before we return it (is it really worth it?). Some people (they are called freeloaders) work very hard to ignore what they owe others. ASD individuals, on the other hand, seem to struggle with understanding this great balance of resource and who is owed what. This is especially true when you move beyond the concrete (e.g., money) into the non-physical (e.g., convenience or emotional support).

I encourage parents of ASD individuals to do what I do to encourage thinking about the experience of others, and then responding in an appropriate way. To the uninitiated, this can feel strange. Also, it should be somewhat contrary to the typical expectations of parents who are supposed to endure hardship silently. Simply stated, you must be explicit about your emotional (e.g., "I'm sad when you say that to me") and physical (e.g., "Losing your bus card so often is becoming a financial burden to the family") experience, and then clearly state how you want your ASD child to respond (e.g., "Apologize to me," "Do extra chores this week to lighten the financial load").

To combat this unintentional ignorance in my own practice, I often ask ASD students to guess what I am thinking and feeling. Most of them are surprised when I tell them (when appropriate) that I am angry, or feel "put out," or am tired of their behavior. I use the line, "The message you are sending me by your behavior is…" I am usually giving them new information. They tell me that the rule they use is that psychologists are happy all the time, or maybe that it did not occur to them that I cared about their actions that did not directly influence me. It usually does not occur to them that I have a complex emotional experience, and it is important to me that others see them as the good people they are. I have to explicitly tell them this, and usually I have to tell them this over and over. Beyond that, I ask them to guess what others are thinking of them, and then systematically correct or adjust their assumptions. In this way, ASD individuals seem to be able to develop fairly reliable guesses about the experience of others. What is often lacking, however, is the spontaneity of guessing. Without my cue, it does not often occur to ASD individuals to initiate that empathic, TOM process. And the default is a self-centered way of approaching the world. This lack of spontaneous responding, by the way, is noted by Rourke (1995), and seems to mediate a lot of social interactions.

What Others are Looking for in Good People

It is important that you teach your children the behaviors that others judge as "good people behavior." I like to go back to the axiom that good people get better treatment from others. In the same way, people who are not nice often draw negative behavior from others. There is practical value in people judging you as a good person.

I know that being a good person and being thought of as a good person can be two different things. It is your job, as the parent, to teach your child to be a good person (if you choose to do so, of course). It is certainly not my job to tell you what values to teach your children, what ideology to espouse, or anything like that. It is definitely my job to help train your child to be thought of as a good person. Good people, in general, get better treatment. Good people are thoughtful, caring, interested in the experience of others, generous and charitable, and polite. Good people also have proper hygiene, smell nice, wear nice clothes, and make good eye contact. Good people have solid handshakes and polite verbal greetings. Good people are strong communicators, and communication is really the key of being thought of as a good person. One must consciously act, and in a certain way, in order to be judged positively. One must take actions that are considered thoughtful (give gifts to their father on Father's Day), be caring (offer to go the store when your mother is feeling ill), be interested in the experience of others (ask people about their day), be generous and charitable (volunteer at an animal shelter), and be polite (always say thank you). Looking the part (proper hygiene and steady eye contact) just makes it easier for people to judge you positively. The opposite presentation (foul smelling, old, raggedy clothes) makes it harder for people to like you.

When parents teach their children how to act like a good person, and insist on certain behaviors that others will judge as good, they are making an investment in the future of their children. These parents are making it easier for their children to get jobs in the future, make friends, find a romantic partner, get a warning instead of a ticket, and get upgraded to business class on an airplane. It should be noted that very few people in general come to this conclusion (i.e., it is better for me when people think I am a good person, and these are the things I need to do to be judged as such) on their own.

ASD teens often ask if they can simply do those behaviors as a way of getting what they want. They wonder if it is simply sufficient to act like a good person instead of both being and acting like a good person. It is true that some people are able to trick others into thinking they are good people when really they are out to take advantage of them. These are often called scam artists. In my experience, ASD teens (and most people, really) are unable to fool others in this way. Acting good without being good almost always looks strange, and I confidently tell the ASD teens I work with that they will always be discovered if they attempt to fool people in this way.

Morality and Logic

Logic is a funny thing. Most of the ASD teens I work with can perform thought processes that are logical. The problem is that most of them arrive at a false conclusion by logical means. They also resist my more correct conclusion because of the firm belief in the process of logic. What they do not understand is that there are a number of factors that influence the course of logic. One of them, explained above, is experience. With increased experience, our "leaps" in logic tend to be shorter (increasing their accuracy) and happen less often (because we have access to more facts).

Morality, and specifically the ability to understand the needs and experience of others, is another major influence in reasoning and logic. One challenging activity for ASD teens is to hold more than one conflicting view in mind at the same time. I think this deficit is related to both the cognitive rigidity ("I'm right and you disagree, so therefore you must be wrong") ASD individuals experience, as well as Executive Functioning deficits (holding multiple pieces of information in the working memory at a time). It is very important to me that my ASD students accept several elements of reality:

- They can be wrong.

- Others can be right when they, themselves, are wrong.

- Their views can and will change over time based on:

  ◦ physiological maturity of their brains

  ◦ experience.

- Sometimes there is no "correct" answer.

- As they age, black and white will decrease, gray will increase.

I am very interested in my ASD students being comfortable with ambiguity and not knowing. After all, it is the pursuit of knowledge and information that inspires the greatest discoveries of mankind (even if their discovery was not what they were originally looking for). For all these reasons, I do a relatively simple exercise with all of my students, several times a year. We participate in a moral dilemma discussion. I believe moral dilemmas are challenging for all individuals, and suitable for instruction, but are especially good for our students because they teach and stress all of the statements above.

One of the more famous moral dilemmas is the Heinz Dilemma:

A woman was near death from a special kind of cancer. There was one drug that the doctors thought might save her. It was a form of radium that a druggist in the same town had recently discovered. The drug was expensive to make, but the druggist was charging ten times what the drug cost him to produce. He paid $200 for the radium and charged $2000 for a small dose of the drug. The sick woman's husband, Heinz, went to everyone he knew to borrow the money, but he could only get together about $1000, which is half of what it cost. He told the druggist that his wife was dying and asked him to sell it cheaper or let him pay later. But the druggist said, "No, I discovered the drug and I'm going to make money from it." So Heinz got desperate and broke into the man's store to steal the drug for his wife. Should Heinz have broken into the laboratory to steal the drug for his wife? Why or why not? (Kohlberg 1981)

Nearly every time I do this exercise I get some similar responses. Some students almost always focus on the particulars. Why $200? Why charge ten times as much? Is Heinz related to the Heinz family that makes ketchup? Where in Europe is this happening? I respond to all of these questions with the same general answer: these questions are loopholes (lines of questioning and reasoning that do not move the discussion forward) and the answers to the questions are irrelevant and counterproductive. The next phase is when the students generate solutions. Every time I do this, at least one person argues that the druggist should cut Heinz some slack. The druggist is being mean, money-grubbing, or should go to jail. I remind the children that in our capitalist economy people have the right to charge what they think is a fair price, and how can you know that the druggist himself did not fall on hard times and needs the money? Ultimately, I tell them, it does not matter what the druggist charges. The point is that Heinz cannot pay and must make a tough decision.

At this point the children begin to get frustrated. They argue with the process and complain that there is no way to win this debate. It is at this moment that I come back to the original point of the moral dilemma and remind them that if there was a right answer, this would not be a moral dilemma. Their job is not to find a solution, but go through the process of reasoning. In fact, I make them argue one side (e.g., Heinz is totally justified in stealing as the life of his wife is at stake) and then right away argue the opposite (e.g., if one person is allowed to steal, who else should be allowed to steal? The Slippery Slope argument).

We split into teams. I introduce the role of Devil's Advocate and make people take turns. I force students to make only unique arguments, ban them from addressing the arguments of others directly, insist they use facts only, insist they use the impassioned plea only, argue with the values of Gordon Gekko, argue with the values of Gandhi, and so on. Quite possibly, the most valuable tool I use is to insist they argue against themselves. After they state an opinion, I ask them to state the opinion of someone who disagrees with them. All of these activities do truly promote flexibility and perspective-taking. The students discover that reasonable people can disagree on important things. This task also introduces doubt as an asset. There is high value in thinking, "I could be wrong about this." Doubt, in this case, promotes humility which leads to a whole set of behaviors that others find good. Our students hopefully begin to see that right and wrong are somewhat flexible, and sometimes unknowable, and it is engaging in the process of finding out that is valuable to society.

If you are thinking this sounds like fun, or something you would like to do more formally with your child, here are a few things you can try. First, look up "moral dilemma" online to come up with some classic dilemmas like the Heinz Dilemma to discuss. Talk these over during dinner or in the car and make it a game or a challenge. Another thing parents tell me they find invaluable is listening to the news in the car when they are driving their child around, and asking them what they think about current events. Parents who just start to do this note they have to be very specific with their questions in the beginning ("Do you think the president/prime minister is doing a good job?"), but when their child gets used to the process, they can be more general ("What do you think of the government's record on immigration?"). Parents also do well to share their own beliefs and thoughts about those events with their children. Manageable doses of moral reasoning and debate (and especially having your child make an argument that is opposite to their own beliefs) over the long term typically results in a child with more flexible thought processes and more openness to the experience of others.

CHAPTER 8

THE ADOLESCENT FIXATION, BEING STUCK, AND THE FREEZE RESPONSE

It is a core tenet of Behaviorism that there is no such thing as random behavior. All behavior is inspired; all behavior comes from a discernible source. Perhaps where I differ from others is that I have the means and the drive to discern most behavior I do not understand right away. Although behavior might not follow rules we recognize, it does follow a pattern.

A class of unusual behaviors I have witnessed from Autism Spectrum Disorder (ASD) individuals can be filed under brainstem behaviors, or behaviors that require very little learning or rehearsal. I will not go into the neurology of these behaviors, and I have not personally studied these behaviors in the sense of looking at fMRIs while they are happening. I am using the term brainstem more in a metaphorical sense than biological sense, and to identify a behavior that seems to me to be based more on instinct and less on learning.

Fight, Flight, or the Other Thing

Did you know that there was another "F" word in the fight or flight options of response to environmental threats? Freeze. When I first saw it happening in a person, I did not know what I was seeing. Fight, flight, or freeze are behavioral responses we inherited from our ancestors that we use when we are presented with an environmental threat. The classic example is the caveman getting attacked by a saber-toothed tiger. Instinctively, we have a response that addresses the situation in a way that preserves our lives. It is the case that this response is automatic and does not happen at the level of conscious awareness (we don't think about it and mull it over before acting). In this sense, it truly is a brainstem response, like a reflex, which is a good thing because in the time it takes us to weigh all of the options and come up with the best response we would likely be mauled by the tiger. You can imagine that those cavemen who did not have the fight, flight or freeze response happen at the level of the brainstem were selected out of the gene pool. Being able to perform some actions (e.g., reflexes) without having to contemplate them is a good thing. Very adaptive.

The "deer in the headlights" phrase is a description of the freeze response, and I do not ever recall seeing this response personally (I had certainly seen it on TV) until I started working with ASD individuals. I had a student who was misbehaving in one of my social skills classes, and I eventually removed him from the classroom (incorrectly guessing that his misbehavior was intended to serve the purpose of gaining attention). I asked him to sit outside the classroom, and he promptly fell asleep. I could not justify stopping the lesson again to go out and wake him up, so I waited until the end of the class to have a talk with him. One of the many downsides of my decision was that I became more and more angry as the minutes wore on and he got a nice little nap. I remember when I let the class out for the end of the period he promptly woke up (he was sleeping near the door), stretched, and made a comment about how good he felt after his nap.

I lost it. This student was taller than me, and I felt I needed a show of force to tell him I was not to be trifled with (I had just come out of working in a boys' group home with children with behavioral disorders) so I got right up in his face. With a calm voice, I asked him what he thought he was doing disrespecting me and my class like that. Who did he think he was? Did he want to have a discussion with the Principal about this? I went on and on, and he simply stood there and looked at me. His unwavering demeanor and posture only made me more angry, so my rhetorical questioning went on much longer than it needed to. Eventually, I realized what I was doing and took a step back, barked a command to get to class, and left the building to cool down. I spoke about it with my colleagues over the next few days and realized I had probably triggered a freeze response in this student. He was not giving me the cool demeanor to irritate me, he was frozen, and probably because my first act had been to invade his personal space. I sent a sensory storm at him by getting too close, and then talking sternly to him. I think it was too much for him. After I realized all of this I went back and apologized to the student.

I suspect this is what happens to a lot of ASD students when I read in their reports from other schools that they got in trouble for being insubordinate. I think the student felt threatened or overwhelmed and froze up. This was reasonably interpreted by the adult in charge as "stonewalling" (intentionally not responding to a question or request for the purpose of gaining the advantage in an exchange), and the situation escalated from there. Adults think they are giving very simple commands (e.g., come out from under the table, leave the classroom, state your name), but do not realize the ASD teen is frozen and his lack of compliance has nothing to do with the simplicity of the demand.

In my experience, the freeze response has to wear off in the same way that the fight or flight response has to wear off—it takes time to calm down and get back to typical or reasonable functioning and decision-making. My advice to parents is that continuing to make demands or increasing the pressure will only prolong the process. The child is having a brainstem response, and it is happening outside of reason and outside the decision-making process. For their part, parents must calm down, walk away, and come back to the situation when things are more calm. Parents must always come back, though. On the part of the ASD individual the answer is to train one's body to be less reactive in these situations. ASD children who are already anxious in social situations, have sensory sensitivities, or have a high level of general anxiety are more likely to have a maladaptive fight, flight, or freeze response. In cases like these, parents should seek professional help for their child for management of anxiety and Sensory Integration.

Areas of Special Interest

In Chapter 2 I suggest that areas of special interest can easily be defined as a strength of the ASD population, but you might ask why it is such a defining characteristic. Most of the ASD individuals I talk to can recall a slew of areas of interest that started from a very early age. They often recall them fondly or sheepishly, but never do they seem to ask themselves what it was about, or why they were so fixated on dinosaurs. I stated earlier that ASD teens seem especially resistant to reflecting on the past, but I think lack of questioning also suggests that the special area of interest is not considered unreasonable and serves a very distinct and meaningful purpose. I have a couple of guesses about what that purpose, or those purposes, might be.

One theme I hear from ASD individuals when they talk about their life and how they feel about it is control, or the distinct feeling of lack of control. They tell me that, especially in social situations, it feels like everyone is speaking a language that they cannot decipher. People seem to know what others mean, or get more information out of discussions than they do. People make jokes that others find funny, but they do not. They have a hard time telling when people are exaggerating or lying. They can become the target of bullying due to their gullibility. In response to this, I think the area of interest could present one item, one aspect of their lives, that makes sense and helps them also make sense of the world around them (see next paragraph). The area of interest offers the ASD individual a chance to master something; to know more about that thing than anyone else. It can form the foundation of interpersonal interactions (allow me to tell you about my special area of interest: hot air balloons; did you hear this new thing about hot air balloons?).

More specifically, Uta Frith described the Weak Central Coherence Theory in the 1980s (Happé and Frith 2006). She suggested that individuals on the Spectrum have trouble understanding context and big-picture thinking, and might use areas of special interest and repetitive behaviors as a way to provide context to thought and to make sense of the world around them. Seeing things in context is so natural to people that most do not even notice that their brain does this process effortlessly. We have an experience and discern what it means all the time. ASD individuals have a hard time with this process, and I suspect being unable to see context can be confusing for them. Enter the special area of interest: this cognitive and psychic toe-hold upon which the rest of their understanding of the world is built.

Areas of interest also seem to offer a chance for the process of mental rehearsal (e.g., reciting lists of Pokémon characters) to ASD individuals. I know that ASD individuals do a lot of mental rehearsal because many of them verbalize it. Regardless of how many times a day I see some students at the school where I work, they will say hello to me each time I see them. We also can have endless conversations about their area of interest that include exactly the same information. There seems to be something comforting and grounding about the process of mental rehearsal. There can also be a downside to this rehearsal. I have had ASD individuals in my office who have chosen as their area of interest how people have treated them poorly or victimized them. More than once I have forbidden a client to ever talk about the list of people who had wronged them that they had been compiling from their childhood to now. I tell them I will not listen to it or tolerate the rehearsal in my office, and I encourage their parents to do the same. Rehearsal of this type of information (my grievances) can inspire anger and resentment that takes root in a person's psyche and inhibits healthy interpersonal functioning and thinking. Interestingly, each time I have forbidden such type of verbal rehearsal, the individual has found something else to talk about with me (and think about), and that anger and resentment seems to loosen and go away over time.

Stuck

Parents tell me that there comes a point in a discussion when their child is not frozen, but they are stuck in a line of reasoning or thinking that is both absurd and intractable. What does it mean to be "stuck"? The best way I can describe it is that it is thinking that resembles a skipping record. I believe that the "stuckness" is often the result of anxiety or otherwise being too worked up and dysregulated. A line of linear thought or reasoning ($A + B + C + D... = N$) gets interrupted because of being blindsided (I wasn't expecting this), being wrong (incorrect information), feeling like you are not being understood, or any other number of unexpected changes in a situation. When an ASD child is stuck, parents know that the answer is rarely to talk it through. Parents find that trying to process or reason through this "stuckness" can take a very long time, and walking away and coming back to the discussion later is equally as effective.

This is actually what I recommend to parents. I coach them to say to their teen, "You are stuck right now. We will talk about this again in 30 minutes." And then walk away. When I do this with ASD teens, they sometimes follow me and try to argue with me. Since I do believe this is a physiological state of upset that is getting in the way of productive thinking and reasoning, giving the physiological state time to return to normal should mean that the thinking and reasoning then will be more productive. More often than not, if the parent walks away and comes back to the issue when things have calmed down (20–30 minutes of peace), talks can resume. I have had little to no success trying to talk or reason ASD individuals out of being stuck. It is not how being stuck works.

Saying, "You're stuck right now," and walking away can be a challenge for most parents. A conversational strategy I learned years ago is called "signposting." Signposting is telling someone right away what to expect and sticking to the most important details. Great storytellers can signpost. They get the listener eager to hear the end of the story and stick with the delivery even when things get boring or bogged down with detail in the middle. I do a form of signposting with ASD individuals when they are stuck. I tell them that I cannot or will not talk about their issue at this moment, but will be happy to talk with them in 30 minutes, or first thing the next day. More often than not, scheduling time to talk about the pressing issue is sufficient to help the teen relax about the immediacy of the need and go on about their lives. In this same way they tend to calm down about the issue, and then you are both dealing with an annoyance rather than a crisis when you come back to it.

Some adults (usually school administrators) like to unintentionally take advantage of a time when an ASD student is stuck to instruct the student on who is in control. The adult incorrectly interprets the ASD individual's stuck-state as stubbornness. I have already mentioned that I think being stuck is largely the result of a heightened physiological state of arousal causing the needle of reasoning and thinking to skip, so it is definitely not a tactic ASD teens use to gain the upper hand in an argument. If you treat it that way, though, several important things will happen.

First, if there is a disagreement, it will always escalate. The stuck ASD teen has no idea that you think they are being stubborn, malicious, or insubordinate. You are fighting two different fights. You will be forced to up the ante, and likely end up at the ultimatum stage before you know it. Ultimatums are almost always a losing strategy with the ASD teen. In my experience, when an ASD teen is given an ultimatum, it seems almost as if they are driven to follow through on the threat (even though you have likely made it easy for them to avoid it). Knowing that the risk of whatever horrible punishment is out there within their reach seems to drive ASD teens to seek it out. It is possible that inviting the inevitable helps restore a sense of control.

Second, you will be left with a choice. Do you follow through on your foolish ultimatum, or do you concede and essentially be the person to blink first. I assure you, to the ASD teen, it is not a contest. For that reason, you will always lose. My best advice is to avoid ultimatums altogether. Get good at walking away and coming back to the discussion. Remember that most ASD individuals are driven by a desire for peace and are rarely out to get other people or make you look bad in front of the other teens and your peers.

Self-assessment, and Avoiding "Better"

"This is how I feel now and it is how I have always felt and always will feel. Do something," is a phrase I commonly hear from my ASD clients. Self-assessment (answering the question, "How are you?") is a challenge for ASD individuals. First, knowing yourself and assessing yourself, and especially your internal state, is tough for most people. Second, reporting out in a way that others find meaningful and informative is a challenge as well. When ASD individuals bring to me some sort of complaint about psychic or physical disturbance or discomfort it can be a challenge to intervene in a helpful way.

Most of the time it takes me a while to figure out what the person is talking about. "I don't feel good, I need to go home," is about all I have to go on sometimes. Describing yourself in a way that allows others to intervene, empathize, sympathize, or have any sort of meaningful reaction is a social skill. You have to know what the other person will find meaningful. To truly understand the experience of your ASD teen, you have to teach them how to give you meaningful information in a reliable way. I have several techniques I use in order to get my ASD students and clients to give me useful information.

At the beginning of every social skills class I lead I have the students answer the question, "How are you feeling right now?" This is the absolutely most important part of the class because I insist they tell me something I can understand that gives me a good amount of information. "Fine" is understandable, but gives me no information. "Sick" gives me information, but I have no idea what it refers to. I push and push to get them to use different words, describe their physical and affective states, give them feedback ("You say you feel happy, but you look very tired and sad right now…"), and make them do it again and again, day after day.

It is also important to teach the skill of scaling. Scaling is simply the process of adding meaningful context to a concept. "Sad" is a concept, and "I feel sad like the time just before I went to the hospital for depression" is a scaled concept. Now I have a better idea of how you are really feeling. In the simplest form, I have teens rate their mood on a scale of zero to ten, where five is an average day. This way the teens have a very convenient, very meaningful way to tell me when they are having a really good day or a really bad day. It can get more sophisticated and personalized from there, but the key is for the child to report their psychic or physical state in a way the listener can understand.

Having the information is not the end in the process. Ideally, we want people to feel like they have some sense of control over how they feel. Professionals also call this sense of control "agency." I get the sense from some of my ASD students and clients that they really do not think about how they feel. Many of them simply feel and react. All of us do this at some time in our life, though. When I am bored I usually go get something to eat. Eating for me is certainly not the most effective way to keep from being bored, and then I feel ill or regretful if I have eaten too much. I cannot say that I pick apart all of my feelings and states and find the best way to react to them, but I certainly have a good idea, as most people do, about the process. Many people with an ASD I talk to describe their internal experience as if it is something that just happens to them with no rhyme or reason, and they must just live with it. "Now I'm sad. I suppose I will be sad until I am happy again," is the sentiment I often hear. They express no sense of agency over their experience (e.g., "I'm sad. Please say something funny").

I want the ASD teens I work with to feel that they have the ability to modify their physical and affective states. I do not want them to feel out of control or disconnected from their experience. Sometimes the hardest part in this process is refusing to solve the problem for the child, even though I know exactly what would help them feel better. Sometimes this means the child will walk away despondent and without a solution, but I am confident when we get to this point that the answer is right around the corner. Humans are, after all, adaptive. When the child responds in an adaptive way, you must be there to initiate the process of reflection. What did they do? What was the outcome? Or, "You look better now. What happened? What did you do after you left my office?" Over and over and over I do this with some children, and over time I see an increase in agency.

The parents of ASD teens I work with report having a hard time figuring out when it is time to step back and let their child regulate their physical and affective states on their own. Some are concerned that their child lacks the skill to adapt, and will go on suffering if they do not step in. Many of these same parents report that they find parent support groups to be helpful. Native Experts can be a huge support to each other both in discerning when it is time to step back and let their child struggle, and when the struggle is too great and they should step in.

Finally, teaching self-assessment right after an intervention is also crucial. I tell my students that it is one thing to apply a reasonable solution, but you have to complete the process and see if it was successful. But I have a secret to impart to you, the parent and Native Expert. If a child comes to you and says he or she is feeling bad and you successfully direct them to generate a reasonable solution, and then you ask them if they feel better, they will, nine times out of ten, respond with "no," even when the visual evidence (improved affect, decreased complaining, brighter complexion) says they do, in fact, feel better. I think most ASD individuals I work with in this process set the standard at feeling their absolute best. Did their intervention or solution cause them to feel the best they have ever felt? But that is not the question that was asked. I have had much more success when doing the follow-up to ask the child, "Do you feel worse?" If the answer is "yes," then that spurs me to come up with a solution for them. They did their part and now I, as the expert, need to step in and help. But if they report, "No, I do not feel worse," I declare success. I tell them that arresting the downward slide is the hardest part and that improvement is right around the corner. For most of the ASD individuals I work with this line of reasoning makes complete sense and is satisfying to them. This line ("Is it worse?") is my gift to you.

Rigidity

Rigidity is more than being opinionated. Rigidity is the imposition of arbitrary rules or parameters on how something must proceed. I think rigidity has a lot to do with comfort and control as well. Rigidity is the imposition of rules (the bastion of safety in an unsafe world) where rules do not apply, or are insufficient. The most simple rule I hear, in various forms, that highlights rigidity is: "I am right and you disagree with me, so therefore you are wrong."

When people talk about rigidity as it relates to ASD individuals, they are usually talking about cognitive rigidity. Anyone can have a strong opinion or strongly held belief, but all can be expected to engage in discourse at the level of being able to see and acknowledge the point of view of someone with a differently held belief. All need to entertain the notion that "it could be otherwise." One of the more frustrating elements of the rigidity associated with ASD individuals is this seeming unwillingness to engage in the process and the discourse. I am not referring to the discourse that results in me seeing things your way. I am talking about discourse where both people want to learn the perspective of the other. Indeed, much of the process of growth and maturation is the consideration of novel and opposing opinions and beliefs.

Everyone has the potential, and sometimes even the drive, to think that they are correct, and will always be correct, but it is my experience that ASD individuals must train themselves, much of the time, to see and entertain the perspective of another, or to see things as being anything other than they appear to be in the moment. ASD teens must be taught to ask themselves, "Is there a better way? Could I possibly be wrong? Will my opinions change in the future?" These are questions we can all entertain to break down our own rigidity. Reflecting on our past and the person we used to be, examining not just victories but also defeats, and believing something someone says because the person is a reliable source, are all activities that break down rigidity.

How does one combat rigidity? Experience, discomfort, contribution, and compromise are the more effective ways to break down rigidity in most individuals. Here are a few of the best ideas I know of for breaking down cognitive rigidity:

- Intentionally mixing things up and making changes and then pointing out that the system, whatever the system is, does not break down. This can be as simple as having breakfast food for lunch and noting that it was a good day anyway.

- Parents have reported to me a lot of success traveling with their children, and specifically seeing other cultures and people groups.

- Doing things that intentionally make people uncomfortable, like going for hikes or day-long walks, sleeping in a hotel bed, taking a car trip without a video game or other distraction (remaining oriented to the social environment), and other activities can all promote flexibility.

- Parents should look for ways they have modified discomfort, negotiation and compromise out of their child's life, and then stop doing this:

  ◦ *Example:* You were so tired of your child complaining about your cooking that you started making two dinners each night; one for the family and one for your ASD child.

  ◦ *Example:* You have decided that getting your ASD child to take out the trash is way harder than doing it yourself and you cannot take one more argument, or do not feel you have the time to micromanage your child.

Making your ASD child's life comfortable at the expense of helping them contribute, experience, and be a part of the family group can often promote rigidity. The opposite action can be an inoculation against rigidity.

PART III

RELATIONSHIPS

CHAPTER 9

SEX, SEXUALITY, AND ROMANTIC RELATIONSHIPS

The Five-year Delay

Autism Spectrum Disorders (ASDs) are more generally categorized as developmental disabilities. I have often recommended parents and other professionals to think of the ASD individual in front of them as being on the emotional level of someone five years younger when it comes to social issues and ways of looking at the world. For instance, TV shows that capture the attention of a 15-year-old with Asperger Syndrome (AS) are often those that capture the attention of a 10-year-old Neurotypical (NT) child. These social delays become most pronounced, I believe, in later school grades where the social rules and social strata are very strict. Indeed, 15-year-olds acting like 10-year-olds can be socially catastrophic, but 25-year-olds acting like 20-year-olds is barely noticeable to most people.

This delay causes an interesting and often volatile conflict when it comes to sex and sexuality. Most ASD individuals, while developmentally delayed, are not physically delayed. All of their physical and hormonal parts mature at the same rate as their NT counterparts. But their cognitive and social parts that are part of sexuality and sexual relationships are on a delayed course of development. It makes me think of that movie *Big* with Tom Hanks. Tom Hanks' character, when he becomes an adult overnight and then gets a job to make ends meet, invites a female co-worker over for a "sleepover." The co-worker is thinking "sleepover" is code for "sex." But to Tom Hanks' character, sleepover is code for sleepover. He calls the top bunk. What is interesting about the movie is that the female co-worker finds Tom Hanks's character's childish behavior (he is literally a child in the body of an adult—high jinks ensue) endearing. She thinks he is in touch with his inner child, naive, genuine, etc. She falls in love with him for this. A 15-year-old managing sexual urges like a 10-year-old, however, can be creepy. Sex, sexuality, and romantic relationships for the ASD population may benefit from some management by you, the parent.

The Meaning of Romantic Relationship

For a number of years I saw little if any dating behavior among the ASD population at the school where I worked. I usually find dealing with teen romance boring, so this was a welcome break. All of a sudden, though, it seemed, students started pairing up. I saw more hand-holding, book-carrying, and "sitting next to each other every chance we can get" behavior. There were two interesting differences that I saw between the teen romances I remembered from my own past and my work in other schools, and the teen romances I saw at this school. First, teens were just as likely to be in same-sex romances as opposite-sex romances. Second, the constant posturing, advancement and retreat, and physical tussle (e.g., boys trying to put their arms around girls) that marks teen romances as one individual tries to increase physical intimacy while the other defends against it, was generally absent in these ASD relationships.

There are lots of reasons why people establish and maintain romantic relationships. Dynamic and long-term relationships fulfill multiple needs for the couple. Providing a sexual outlet (mentioned above) is just one of the needs romantic relationships can fulfill. Most people develop a sense of identity through their romantic relationships as well. In fact, it can be an emotional boost to think that this other person likes me enough to be seen with me, and spend time and energy on me. At its most base description, romantic relationships can say something about a person's value. Romantic relationships also fulfill that need to "be known" by someone. Your partner is someone who takes an interest in you as a person and spends time getting to know the you that is typically hidden from much of the world. This is the drive I call "affiliation." Partners spend time together with the intention that they are moving toward a deeper understanding and bonding with each other. Indeed, relationships do not just stagnate, but they dissolve when one or both members decide to go no deeper with the other.

I spent some time working in a middle school several years ago. Remember, this is the age of children I am looking at to understand the ASD teen romantic relationship. Sixteen-year-old ASD teens who pair up should be looked at like 11-year-olds. Eleven-year-olds certainly do date, but not for the reason that 16-year-olds date. When you see middle-school-age girlfriends and boyfriends, you rarely (thank god) see any sense of sexual tension or overtly directed sexual energy. What you see are efforts to influence a person's social status and reputation. In my experience, the main reason middle-schoolers pair up is to be cool and popular. That is it. It has little if anything to do with sex drive as that is still largely dormant at that age (except in extraordinary circumstances that are outside the purview of this book). Getting a girlfriend or boyfriend in the middle-school grades is one of the best ways to change one's status. Interestingly, the girlfriend does not even have to be real. It can be a girl that you tell your friends is from Canada that you met on summer vacation. Middle-schoolers are also not wise to the ways of the world.

The romantic relationship, whatever the intent, is actually a very challenging style of relationship. They are difficult relationships for everyone—from the couple going on their first date to the couple celebrating their 50th anniversary. Romantic relationships never get easy. What does one talk about with this person whose interests are so different from mine? What do I do with my hands while we are standing and talking? Do we walk side by side? If socializing is not a simple activity for the ASD individual, socializing with a person from another gender in the context of a romantic relationship is harder still. When I watch these ASD couples interact, I get the sense that they are sometimes trying to act the way they *think* couples *should* act. I get the sense that little of it feels comfortable and most of it feels foreign, at least until they get into a routine or rhythm. I have described these romantic relationships, in fact, as an approximation of a romantic relationships. These teens have likely seen countless examples on TV, movies, and the internet of couples in romantic relationships, and when I observe them it feels much like they are acting out scenes. Consequently, this is a bit how 11-year-olds are with "trying things on," so to speak.

This is, of course, not the case for all such relationships. My original goal is to describe and interpret what I am seeing in the hopes it will give you, the Native Expert, a clue as to what your ASD teen might be experiencing. The next question to ask, however, is what would be the purpose in setting up this approximation of a romantic relationship? I do get the sense when I talk to these teens that they could really take or leave the romance part. Go back to the status issue, though. A romantic relationship can provide someone with credentials. I believe it gives the ASD teens credentials, but not necessarily just with their peers. Unlike NT teens, I get the sense that their ASD peers do not care one way or another who is dating whom. Like I said, exclusivity is not a hallmark of these relationships. Dating among ASD teens rarely ever dictates who each individual in the relationship can and cannot hang out with the way it does with NT teens.

Many of the teens I work with lament (overtly or subtly) the loss of normalcy (e.g., "I am not like the average teen"). In my experience, this usually happens in high school grades. ASD students at this stage will tell me that they want to go to a typical school and attend football games, go to parties and concerts, and do all the "cool school stuff" that teens on TV are doing. I think it is probably really hard to be a teenager on the Spectrum because they are just getting a better sense of what is considered normal, and just how far their own experience diverges from normal. One way I think these teens fight to achieve some sort of normalcy or typicality is to get a romantic relationship. This is not always the case, but ASD teens pairing up is often my cue to ask if everything is okay with them. I ask them how they feel about their diagnosis, how they feel about attending a "special school" or being in a special program at school. They often tell me that they would like more friends who are not on the Spectrum or that their classmates annoy them and they want to go to a different school.

In these cases, parents would do well to speak to adults working with their ASD teen who know them well, such as a school teacher, Boy Scout leader, or adult family friend. Parents can ask if there has been any change in behavior (e.g., work production, irritability) or relationships (e.g., "Do they have a girlfriend, or someone they are hanging out with more?", "Do they seem more isolated and withdrawn than usual?"). Parents will also do well to inquire of their ASD teen directly. Ask them about how they are feeling about their diagnosis, their specialized program at school (if applicable), or how they are getting along with others. Again, ASD teens seem to be remarkably open and honest when the question is asked correctly (e.g., correct wording, good timing, more positive mood).

Supportive Parents

Most healthy romantic intentions do follow the linear path from "What can you do for me?" to "What can I do for you?", and romantic maturity is not guaranteed for anyone. I think that, like all other social activities and drives, romantic relationships do change and mature for the average ASD individual. I know many ASD adults who are in relationships they find emotionally fulfilling and meaningful, sexually healthy, and dynamic. Some ASD adults I know in romantic relationships have partners who are also on the Spectrum, and some who are not. Some ASD adults have little to no motivation to be in a long-term romantic relationship, while some desire to have one but do not want to go through the hassle and maintenance of having one. Some ASD adults seem driven to relate exclusively for the purpose of having children and creating a family. To me, the romantic potential of an ASD adult sounds much like that of a non-ASD adult.

Many parents do not know how to react when they see that their ASD child has a boyfriend or girlfriend. Most tell me they had no idea their child even noticed the opposite gender existed, and certainly never thought about sex with another person. At the very least, what they are seeing does not usually resemble what they remember from when they were at school.

I recommend to most parents who ask me for some context and meaning to their child's experience that they think about the romance of their ASD teen more like a middle-school romance. Many parents tell me this helps them guess what is going on and anticipate changes more accurately. My primary advice to parents in this situation is that the parents I see that are the most happy and least stressed are those who have decided not to fight the fact that their child is in a romantic relationship (no matter how unfamiliar that relationship might be). Acceptance not only puts you on the path to reduced stress, but it also makes you a potential ally for your child. The line I like to use with teens who ask me for dating advice, which you can use and put in your own words, is the following:

> I think teen romances are a bad idea [this is actually my true opinion]. I have seen little good come from them relative to the potential harm and hardship and I recommend you break up and focus instead on your school work. I do, however, know that you will disregard my advice and keep dating this person. I want you to know that I will support you in any way that I can. I want you to be happy, safe, and healthy, so if there is anything I can do for you, or any way I can advise you in this relationship, please let me know.

If you think teen romances are a great idea, then feel free to substitute your own reason for why this particular relationship should end. Maybe you do not like your child's partner. Maybe your child's grades are poor and they really cannot afford the time for the relationship. Get creative, but be genuine. Even though I tell the teen I think they are making a mistake and a bad choice, they always come and ask me for help when the relationship (inevitably) turns bad. The Native Expert knows this relationship will be hard and will most likely end terribly. You have the option to be there, in a crucially supportive role, by saying to your child what I say to them. These teens understand my sentiment, and they know where to go when it gets tough because I have told them to come to me.

See this as an opportunity to teach your child about social skills, and specifically in romantic relationships. This one will not likely work out, but if they keep at it (and learn from mistakes) there likely will be one that does work out. Talk about traditional dating activities like going to see a movie and why people choose that for a first date (shared experience, little uncomfortable conversation, don't have to look at the other one too much). Talk about being polite and respectful, and what happens when you are not. Talk about the phases of a relationship, and how humans normally move toward exclusivity and commitment in romantic relationships. This romantic relationship is opening up to you, the parent, a whole new category of rich discussion and learning about socializing and relationships that you need to exploit.

Finally, if there is one thing these ASD teens do well it is being honest and frank. Ask them if they are having sex, or how far they have gone physically. Ask them if they are being safe. Tell them about your expectations for relationships, and safety and respect in those relationships. Their frankness and honesty may surprise you, but it is information you can use for their protection and education. When it comes to high-stakes relationships and interactions like those in romantic relationships, I encourage parents to avoid the "let nature take its course" approach and get a little more involved in setting standards and expectations. In school, romantic relationships are a bad place to exert one's independence and maturity, and your child will benefit from your advice and direction.

Ten-year-old Mentality, 15-year-old Body

Sex and sexuality these days is definitely more than a biological process. If sex were just the thing we did to procreate, this would not be as much of an issue. Sex is, however, relational. In fact, there is far more "relating" in sex than the actual sex act.

Think about the time when you started noticing the opposite gender. Think about the time when you started getting interested in your peers romantically, or had your first celebrity crush. From that moment on, your crush, and the feelings and urges associated with it, colored and directed just about every interaction you had with that person, or others like that person. Sexuality permeates the average school gathering of teens. Boys posture to impress girls, girls do the same for boys. We can trace these sexually charged interactions back to the most humble beginnings of society.

To understand the experience of your ASD teen, take all of the drive of sexuality and eliminate any amount of understanding you had about it, any camaraderie or sense of belonging to a group of like-minded individuals (e.g., your friends) with similar drives, and any clue as to the steps one takes to go from the drive to some potential satisfaction of that drive and you have a better understanding of your ASD teen. Even if you felt clueless as a teen about sex, you likely had some peer group who were equally clueless or misinformed. What is different about the ASD teen experience, however, is a seeming lack of frustration or concern about not understanding the drive or the disconnect or inability to discern the social aspect of sexuality. Most ASD teens I talk to about managing their sexual urges do not seem to be particularly distressed by their urges, or their relative difficulty in parlaying them into an age-appropriate romantic relationship.

More than once I have had to tell a teenage ASD boy to cover his erection, and, at the very least, not to do full body stretches while wearing sweat pants while having one. Upon questioning them they report that it does not even occur to them that others can see them doing this. Other boys have had to get coached about not staring directly at the chests of girls in their class. Girls, on the other hand, sometimes need coaching on the message they send to boys when they dress in revealing clothes, or flirt with boys and then become incensed when the boy asks them on a date. These teens often need to hear, "Your sexuality is showing," and they need specific direction on what to do with it.

If you wonder if your ASD teen has urges, wonder no more. They absolutely do. Some of the ASD teens I talk to can label these urges and understand where they come from and what they theoretically need to do about them. Some cannot. Some cannot pair their biological drive with the activity of sex and procreation. Your children are likely somewhere along this spectrum of understanding, but they are not asexual people. They have a sex drive.

The good news, I tell parents, is that your child will likely start dating later than the average NT child. They will also be likely not to have sex until later than the NT child. In fact, it is hard to have sex with someone when your absolute favorite activity is being alone, in your room, playing video games. For NT teens, the drive to affiliate (be in a deep, meaningful relationship) roughly parallels the biological drive for sex. They have semi-complementary social and biological drives. Not so for your child. That social, affiliative drive is the part that is delayed. So where does the biological sex drive go?

What parents need to watch out for is making sure your child's sex drive is not getting your child in trouble or causing a problem for them. Things I have seen an ASD teen's sex drive (unfortunately) encourage them to do include:

- have erections in public that they do not think to conceal

- indiscriminately stare at the bodies of the opposite (or same) sex

- ask questions loudly about sex in public to their parents or me

- get heavily involved with pornography

- get heavily involved with internet pornography communities

- use sexually harassing language with opposite-gender peers or adults

- draw or otherwise create excessive amounts of pornographic art that they do not think to keep to themselves

- look at pornography on borrowed or family computers, or in public

- touch themselves excessively in public or when they are around others (e.g., "adjusting" themselves through their pockets for longer than it should take)

- solicit sexual attention and then accuse the "taker" of harassing them.

Let me be clear, though. As opposed to a sex offender, your child is not doing these things in order to victimize others. I have never seen any malice in these actions. In fact, if your child had any idea how uncomfortable he or she was making others, or how offensive their behaviors were to others, they would stop immediately. But again, discerning that level of offense is a Theory of Mind activity, and not an area where they naturally excel.

There are, of course, the less obvious forms of sexual sublimation. Many ASD girls I know fawn over boy bands long after it is age-appropriate to do so. These 17-year-old girls do not usually look around and notice that all the other girls around them at the Backstreet Boys concert are age 11. They do not notice (or care) that they have moved past the age when jumping and squealing with delight is irritating, but endearing at the same time. Now it is just off-putting and one more way they isolate themselves from their peers. Behaviors that were once cute (wearing bunny ears and tail) when you are age 10 are now interpreted as overtly sexual in older teens. These behaviors send a specific message, but not the one your teen intends to send, and she certainly does not know what to do when boys her age (or older) respond in kind.

As one can imagine, parents who have been confronted with these behaviors in their child report being more than a little embarrassed and concerned. Regardless of how your child directs sexual energy, do not think that sex and sexuality is not an issue for them. Sexual energy must go somewhere. Where is your teen's sexual energy going? Not thinking about it and not addressing it is about the worst choice a parent can make at this point because the risks for making a mistake of misdirected sexual energy (like those I listed above) are only going to become more extreme and severe as your child gets older. At the very least, consult a professional (such as your child's pediatrician) on this issue.

Discussing Sex

I highly recommend talking about sex with your child, even if it is not a problem at this time, or you feel it has been addressed. As I said above, the risks are great, and ever-increasing as a function of age. Have a discussion with your child about what the world and the average person thinks about sex. One activity I do with my students that makes me shake my head each time I do it is ask the group to come up with as many reasons they can think of that people have sex. The first time I did this I think I could come up with five. My students identified 17 reasons in just a couple of minutes. Next, I help them categorize the acts as social, secret, hidden, divisive, or ceremonial to add more context for discussion. Let this discussion evolve and respond to questions exactly as they are presented by the teens. Parents need to get over the taboo we all feel about talking about sex with our children. This discussion will help, and I assure you that you will be way more squeamish than your ASD child. Remember, they likely do not understand much of the social side of sex. Sex to them is mostly a biological process, and there is little reason to be embarrassed about a biological process we all share.

Talk to them about the rules of sex and explain that most people intend eventually for sex to be an activity they share with someone else. Talk about how sex is mostly emotional and relational, and that this means one must spend a lot of time thinking about the feelings and experience of others in order to be successful. Talk about what happens when people break rules, such as staring or gawking at others, or displaying overtly sexualized behavior in public. Talk about the high premium modern society places on mutual respect and empowerment in sexual relationships, and what happens to people who are sexually disrespectful and victimizing. And, of course, talk about safe sex, including diseases and pregnancy. Your child's school may have had this discussion, but they do not know your child like you do, so you need to have it as well.

Parents need to talk with their ASD children (and all of their children for that matter) about how to appropriately and discreetly channel their sexual energy prior to and even while they are in a sexual relationship. I know that the first thing you are thinking is that you are going to have to describe to your child how to masturbate and put a condom on a banana, and that makes you anxious. There are other ways, however, to channel sexual energy. One of the best ones, outside masturbation (which, by the way, you will not likely have to teach your child), is exercise. Regular exercise and physical activity should at least dampen the sexual energy in all people, and especially your child. Yes, another benefit for exercise. Most importantly, however, please warn and correct your child about public displays of sexual energy.

Your child would likely benefit from hearing from you that most people get a girlfriend or boyfriend as much to have someone to have sex with as to have someone on whom to focus one's relational attention. Your child may not choose to go this route, and it is certainly not one I recommend (just going out with people for sex), but they need to become aware of the link between sex and romance. This piece of information could protect them in future relationships.

There are two things I want to warn parents about here. First, and this is true for all children, if you do not educate your child about sex, someone else will. The best sources your child has for information are the internet and each other, and if you are interested in what he or she will learn from the internet about sex, type "sex" into any search engine and check out the first ten listings. That is what they will learn about sex, if you do not tell them. The second point I want to make is that it does not always occur to ASD teens to figure things out or problem-solve when they are confused. If they have questions about sex or their sex drive, a lot of them will simply live with their confusion. This is that self-advocacy piece that is so hard for many of our ASD teens. In this case there may be massive confusion from which you are saving your child. Please address this issue as soon as possible if you have not already.

Sexuality, Gender, and Identity

A topic most parents brace themselves for when their children are teens is that of sexuality. ASD teens are not exempt from questions about their own sexuality. Indeed, I have known plenty of ASD teens who have contemplated their sexuality and sexual preference in order to declare that they were heterosexual, bisexual, homosexual, or even asexual (i.e., preferring no sex and avoiding the sex act altogether). In addition, I have known several ASD teens who made the decision to identify as the opposite of their biological gender.

There are a couple of comments I want to make about the notion of sexuality, gender, and identity. The first is that there is a strong social piece to sexuality and gender. Most people are aware that society has expectations for them, including a set of behaviors that are consistent with their gender (e.g., men must act "manly" and aggressive and be sexually attracted to women, women must be quiet and demure and sexually attracted to men). Modern society is changing rapidly, and especially in the last 50 years, but these stereotypes and expectations still dominate culture.

Second, because your ASD child is less aware of social norms and expectations in general, they are also less aware of society's expectations related to their gender and sexuality. I see the ASD population as a good model for what it looks like when people openly and honestly explore and learn about their sexuality and gender. They are, essentially, uninhibited by society's often unrealistic and overbearing opinions, and are more free to be genuine and exhaustive in their search. Most ASD teens I meet are unconcerned with the gender and sexuality preferences of their peers. They also seem unaware, as opposed to most NT teens, of how the choices of their peers reflect on them. For instance, at nearly every school dance I chaperone there are boys dancing with other boys without any sense of embarrassment or need to explain that they are not gay to their friends.

This exploration of sexuality and gender seems to happen as much in the mind as it does in action. For instance, a very common interaction I have with ASD teens about sexuality can go like this:

Me: So, you told your dad you were bisexual, and your dad wanted me to ask you about that and see if everything was okay. How did you come to that conclusion? How do you know you are bisexual? You told me last week you had never been in a romantic relationship.

Client: Well, when I think about it, I can imagine starting a family with either a boy or a girl. If it turns out to be another boy, we can just adopt kids. Because I do not obviously prefer one gender over the other, I must be bisexual.

Me: Fair enough. Should your dad be worried about you?

Client: What do you mean? Why would my dad be worried?

Me: Because your dad told me you announced at the dinner table that you were bisexual last week, went right back to eating, and haven't said anything about it since then. He's worried there is something you are not telling him.

Client: Oh. No, I'm fine.

This is not to say that ASD teens do not experiment with the behaviors that go along with sexuality or gender, they just do not seem to see the actual behaviors as necessary to identify with a group. For example, they do not necessarily have to get into physical fights to feel like they belong with other boys. Parents should know that just because your ASD teen is not coming out and saying they are gay, or the opposite gender, does not mean they are not contemplating it, and they might have even made a concrete decision one way or the other. Making sure others (like their parents) know how they feel is not always very important or necessary to ASD teens (in fact, it often does not occur to them that others might care). ASD teens also seem to not notice the discrepancy between their statements (e.g., "I am gay") and their behavior (e.g., "I have no interest in dating").

The main point I would like to make regarding sexuality and gender is that exploration of each is actually an exploration of identity. In their teenage years, ASD children are likely actively thinking about who they are and what defines them. I know it is easy for parents to see announcements like "I'm gay" or "I'm really a girl and not a boy" as catastrophic, but I encourage parents to see these announcements as indications of the exploration of identity. Teenagers need to feel like they belong somewhere, and gender and sexuality groups often provide a place to belong.

There is no magic or special skill set involved in talking with your child about sexuality, gender, and identity. Most parents are reluctant to have these discussions because they feel embarrassed, have their own personal horror stories of having the "sex talk" with their parent, or feel their child simply is not ready for such a discussion. Open and honest discussion between parents and their children seems to be one of the most effective ways to build the relationship and promote a sense of safety and security within the family. If you are having trouble getting started with talking about identity issues with your child, look for more detailed resources online or in the bookstore, and go with a strategy that suits your parenting style. If all else fails, let your ASD child's care provider (e.g., teacher, therapist) know that this is a topic you want to discuss with your child and you need help getting started. You will find that once you get started, it certainly does get easier.

CHAPTER 10

VERTICAL RELATIONSHIP MANAGEMENT

Vertical Relationships

As mentioned earlier, noticing, accepting and managing social hierarchy can be a challenge for Autism Spectrum Disorder (ASD) individuals. Most of my ASD students initially reject the notion that there is a social hierarchy in society. The other part that ASD teens, especially, seem to struggle with is the difference between hierarchy and inequality. As I have said previously, our ASD teens seem to place a high value on equality and fairness. The practice of hierarchy looks like some people receive better treatment than others, and I think ASD teens struggle with managing an internal drive that is committed to balance and fairness with the activities of hierarchy and one-way respect (e.g., children can be called by their first name, but must address adults as "Mr." or Ms.").

Convincing ASD teens that adults deserve respect because they are adults, have certain responsibilities, and can do things for us, and not because of anything particularly amazing they have done, can be a challenge. This same reasoning can be applied to bosses, clergy, and teachers, among others. I tell my clients that, in its most basic form, it is considered an accomplishment to stay alive so long, so therefore adults deserve respect. Failing to acknowledge the hierarchy is one thing, though. If a person says they are aware of the hierarchy, but they reject it on the grounds that it is fundamentally unfair, that sounds reasonable to me. That is a thoughtful (although arguably misguided) response. This response is contrasted, however, to that of many ASD teens that seem to have a certain amount of lack of awareness of the hierarchy. When you ask the teen about it, they can talk about it and define and give examples of it, but their behavior often suggests that they are usually just not considering it or understanding how to work with the concept in real time. I will list some of the behaviors below that suggest to me that ASD teens do not have a sense of the fact that we all exist somewhere in a hierarchical social system.

Social Hierarchy

The following is the primer I use for teaching ASD teens about social hierarchy. Everyone exists somewhere on the social hierarchy where we can identify people above us and people below us. There are relatively strict rules governing how we treat people who are not on our tier. Consequently, much of the relationship discussion so far has been about lateral, or peer relationships. More on that later.

At the top of the hierarchy for the ASD teen are bosses, parents, grandparents, and teachers. When a person is interacting with someone above them on the hierarchy, most interactions are marked by formality of behavior and language, and proper manners. In fact, in nearly every interaction you have with someone above you in the hierarchy, you almost cannot go wrong if you use proper manners and formal language. Examples of such universally acceptable language up the hierarchy are things like saying please and thank you, and using more formal titles such as Mr. and Ms. when addressing people.

It is true that certain events and situations will serve to modify the rules when addressing someone above you. For instance, turning 18 officially makes you an adult, but you probably still refer to your friends' parents as Mr. or Mrs. I have seen some parents make managing upward more challenging for ASD teens by letting the teen or their teen's friends call them by their first name. I think this must make the parent feel like they are being less formal, or they think it will make the child feel more comfortable around them, or honor their "coming of age." In my experience, this is confusing for ASD teens. It takes a challenging situation and adds more options or choices. I prefer simpler, more universal standards when managing and teaching appropriate behavior to ASD teens. Situations that have fewer options speed up response and make choosing the most correct response easier. Very few people can fault you for being unnecessarily formal and polite. Also, some people (including ASD teens) hold to the notion that adults must "earn" respect. This concept of earning respect is also confusing, so I give my students the following explanation. There are at least two kinds of respect: earned and unearned. An example of unearned respect is that which a person is owed simply by being alive longer than you.

I suggest that you help your child develop the habit of being polite at all times with everyone who is above them in the hierarchy. This seems to serve everyone better rather than allowing too many options that leave too many opportunities for mistakes. The simpler the skill, by the way, the more transferable. If they treat grandma with respect, they are more likely to treat other elderly people with respect as well.

Down the hierarchy can be a little more challenging. There are a lot of different schools of thought on how we should treat people below us on the hierarchy. Some people believe that they were made tougher and stronger by being treated poorly by people above them, and thus adopt a hazing mentality with people below them. Some choose to utterly ignore people below them. You have likely had bosses that are examples of both extremes. I have two general rules in this case. First, there is no reason I have discovered not to be nice to people. When in doubt, be nice. Second, when there is question about your social standing, consider yourself on the lowest rung of the ladder. There is an old proverb that says, "It is better to consider yourself the least and be elevated to the top than consider yourself the highest and be shamed when you are put back in your place." You cannot be faulted for putting yourself lower on the "ladder."

The reality, I tell my ASD teens, is that teenagers (and especially boys) are at the very bottom rung of society. I use the example of boarding a bus to tell them where they stand in society. I tell them that they should let everyone who is of higher social standing, and those that are awarded preference because of their ability, board the bus in front of them. They should let everyone who is older than them go first, then all the children (because of the nice rule and the ability rule); and then with the teens that are left, all the girls go next (because we believe in this society that females should be shown respect by having preference in certain situations). At that point I encourage them to look around and see who is left. Lest they get despondent, I tell them that time and persistence will earn them a place higher in the hierarchy of society, and that there is a process for this. The fact that these "guidelines" are, in many cases, actual bus rules that you can find written down bolsters my argument.

Universal Rules for Managing the Hierarchy

- Be polite.

- When going up, be formal (*note:* this can backfire when going across the hierarchy).

- Be nice.

- When in doubt, consider others above you on the hierarchy.

Common Mishaps

There are two general categories of mistakes that ASD teens make when navigating the social hierarchy. The first is treating adults or people above them in the hierarchy as equals. There are times when I get the sense that the teen actually believes the individual above them is put there falsely, and that they are actually better and should be higher than that person (I call this acting like the "Little Prince"), but this is more the exception and does not often happen. More than likely when an ASD teen artificially lowers a person's role in the hierarchy it is because they are failing to recognize the hierarchy. Examples of such behavior are things like correcting teachers when they share seemingly false information, not checking in with bosses and supervisors when work is complete, and even failure to make eye contact with a person of authority. My absolute favorite behavior that marks this failure of recognition is the use of the phrase, "Well, actually..." Many of my students will attempt to correct my "mistake" or oversight by beginning their retort to my statements with "Well, actually..." and then a comment about how I could have been more accurate in my commentary. Much of the behavior can come across as conceited (ASD teens can sometimes be seen as arrogant), dismissive, or pompous. Despite how it comes across, I will say again that more often than not this behavior comes from a failure to recognize hierarchy.

There is no end to the trouble that this type of behavior can bring on an individual. The problem with it is that adults are already primed, because of the general reputation of teens, to be disrespected by them; adults anticipate disrespect. An ASD teen comes along with his or her arsenal of annoyances (the "Well, actually...", shifty eyes, and dismissive tone) and adults cannot help themselves but exert their authority. The problem is that the ASD teen rarely understands what is happening when they are sent to the Principal's office, or put in the back of the police car for being unintentionally disrespectful.

The other general category of mistake is treating someone on the same level of the hierarchy (called a "peer") as if they were below you. Interestingly, it is the same arsenal of annoyances described above that I have seen get ASD teens in so much trouble with their peers. The largest single category of behaviors that taunts and annoys peers seems to be this "Well, actually..." behavior. Most ASD teens have at least one area of interest where they have an inordinate amount of knowledge, or at least believe they are the expert. Most ASD teens have a number of these areas, and generally have a large store of facts in their brains. It is not hard to wander on to a subject that activates one of these stores of knowledge, and then comes the competition of information with the peer. No one likes to be corrected, and especially not by a peer who is not a close friend. Failure to recognize the hierarchy in this case (treating peers like they are your disciples or students) tends to lead to isolation or actual torment. Teens tend to stay away from other teens who annoy them. In worst-case scenarios, they target these annoying peers for torment and bullying.

When Honesty and Convention Collide

When equality, honesty, and frankness guide your social interactions, as they do for many ASD teens, some of what goes on in the world does not make sense. For instance, it makes little sense to many ASD teens why they should not immediately, boldly, and in front of the class correct the teacher in the moment when he or she shares incorrect, or less than perfectly correct, information with the class. ASD students tell me all the time that they felt it would be unfair to the rest of the class if they allowed that false information to just linger out there, falsely informing their peers (who they see now as underlings since they did not notice the mistake the teacher made). The answer is that our society is more dependent on the maintenance of the social hierarchy than it is on most things (like absolute correctness of information in lessons). For this reason, I take every opportunity to have the "this is how it is in society" discussion with my ASD students and clients. The Native Expert will note, however, that not everyone sees it as their role to teach the ASD teen a life lesson with every interaction, and especially not when that teen is being annoying or dismissing.

For this reason, I advocate for the intervention my grad-school professor told me never to do. I recommend the Native Expert to occasionally make the response to the question, "Why must I do/not do this?" from their ASD child, "Because I said so." Even though there is a perfectly reasonable and logical explanation for why we do most everything, expecting immediate access to that level of reasoning, as well as a cultural interpreter (someone to explain how we got here, and why everyone seems to be on the same page with this standard), is not realistic. ASD teens can have a hard time performing a task they do not understand but interpret as unreasonable. The point is, however, that one should not be dependent on understanding the reasoning behind an expectation to fulfill an expectation. I am sure you, the Native Expert, can name several times a day you fulfill someone's expectation without knowing or caring, really, what the point is. This is not to say that the point or reason is unknowable, but knowing is not necessary to productivity and compliance. Judicious use of the phrase "Because I said so" can inoculate your ASD child from the drive to know before doing. This is a hugely adaptive trait, and I recommend it especially to parents who love to engage their children in the "why" question. Some parents I meet love having lengthy conversations with their children about the purpose of putting your dishes in the sink, or the benefits of studying math when your intention is to pursue writing, or why someone would vacuum and dust the house when they had the money to pay someone else to do it. To these parents I encourage you to weave into your discourse "Because I said so" moments. If you do not, I guarantee you that someone else will.

Strategic Conformity

I give full credit for the idea of advocating social conformity to ASD students to my colleague Olivia Flint, who was teaching social and independent living skills to a class of 10th graders. One student asked her why they had to learn about proper dress etiquette in the workplace, and she embarked on a journey of explanation that was summarized in the following explanation: "We all need to make money so we can buy things we want and need. You will get a job so you can trade your skills and labor for that money. You will find it much easier to get someone to hire and pay you if you learn to strategically conform to their expectations."

There are a lot of rules governing our interactions and social exchanges. Following those rules does not necessarily mean you have to change who you are or what you believe. Success can sometimes be the process of strategically picking and choosing the rules that get you where you want to go. Getting what you want always involves compromise. Nothing comes without a cost, and the cost is more personal and direct as one approaches and enters adulthood. Having trouble understanding the relative value of things (a common problem in ASD individuals) can make understanding this exchange much more difficult.

Top 10 Relational Mistakes at School and Work

The following is based on my experience working with ASD individuals. There are a number of things I always talk about with my students when they are about to go out into public and represent their school. These pearls of wisdom are based on mistakes I have seen happen time and again:

1. *Correcting your boss or teacher.* There is nothing that can help you fall out of grace and favor faster than this. Happy bosses can make the job great; unhappy bosses can make the job torture.

2. *Failing to check in with your peers to see if they are interested in what you are saying.* Most nice people will not walk away from a boring conversation, but this is what is required of teachers sometimes with ASD individuals. It would be great if I were occasionally asked, "What do you think?" or "Are you interested at all in what I am saying?" by my students, but that rarely happens. I have trained myself, the moment I get bored, to say, "I have no interest in what you are talking about. Either change the subject or I am going to walk away from you." This may seem offensive, but is consistent with the need for direct instruction of social skills.

3. *Telling on a peer.* Also called "ratting someone out" or "snitching," suggesting that the person who tells is a rat, or lower form of life. It is very challenging for the ASD teen to figure out when they should let misbehavior or injustice go (i.e., those times when pointing it out will make things worse) and when they should address it. I encourage my ASD students to avoid pointing out wrongdoing in public, but wait until a person in authority is alone and approach them subtly with the issue. Wrongdoing can activate this sometimes obsessive sense of justice in ASD individuals, but telling on someone can also make one a target of bullying.

4. *Refusing to do an activity.* ASD teens often do not realize that suggestions from people above them in the hierarchy are rarely suggestions. I had a student who was given two tasks: shred a pile of documents and sweep the front steps. Her boss stated it like this: "When you are done with the shredding, you could sweep the front steps if you like." The girl shredded the documents and then decided she would rather read a book than sweep the front steps. It is true that the literal interpretation of the phrase made the sweeping optional, but because of the source (a person above her in the hierarchy), it was automatically considered an order. Parents will get better compliance when they make their expectations clear, but your ASD child also needs to be prepared for the case that ambiguous and seemingly optional orders are not actually optional.

5. *Failing to self-advocate in the form of seeking clarity.* ASD individuals have a strange relationship with ambiguity. First, because of the problem with interpreting non-verbal language and non-literal meaning of words (i.e., pragmatic language), I would suspect they encounter more situations that seem ambiguous than Neurotypical (NT) people. Second, when they discover ambiguity, there seems to be a reluctance to seek clarity, or simply an acceptance that the correctness of their interpretation is based on chance (e.g., "Hope I'm right…"). Knowing when to ask for clarity and when to figure it out on your own is an extremely complex task, and one that takes a lot of trial and error and knowledge of the source of the help (e.g., the teacher). It is not uncommon for ASD individuals to choose an all-or-nothing approach (i.e., never ask for help, never stop asking for help).

6. *Sexually harassing a co-worker or peer.* I have addressed this earlier in the book, but there is an expressive side to pragmatic language. Looking at something too long (like a co-worker's chest) is a form of communication called "gawking" or "leering." It is almost universally seen as inappropriate, and most formal environments (the workplace, school) have rules against it. Discussing sexually themed topics in public, regardless of who it is directed at, is also a very risky endeavor. Our ASD teens often miss the severity of these issues and behaviors because their intention is rarely ever to victimize others when they are doing them. Minus the intent, they often do not understand or sense the inadvertent offense.

7. *Falsely accusing a co-worker or peer of sexual harassment.* This issue is a minefield for me, so I do not want ever to suggest that if your child accuses someone of sexual harassment, or misinterprets an actual statement or action (or any kind of harassment, for that matter), that they are making a false claim. What I do know is that ASD teens I have talked to have very little sense of what happens if they mistakenly make such a claim. Our society takes (or should take) these claims very seriously, and the life of the accused changes from the point of the accusation. Harassment is not a claim to make

lightly because the burden of proof is usually on the accused (as opposed to our more typical "innocent until proven guilty" mentality).

8. *Dominating group discussions.* Workplaces seem to love to get everyone together for the purpose of talking things through. Sometimes there are weekly (or more frequent) staff meetings. Most workers learn quickly that staff meetings are boring and no one wants to be there, and that the less they talk the faster the meetings go (and sooner they end and everyone can go back to work). I have seen plenty of ASD teens and young adults in these types of meetings miss the non-verbal glares of their co-workers, and the uncomfortable shifting of their supervisors as they talk well past their (unstated) allotted time in such meetings. When I follow up with these ASD individuals and ask them what they were thinking, their response is usually that they had a lot to say on the subject, and it was okay because no one else was speaking up. I try to help these individuals set up speaking limits (e.g., limited number of comments, speaking only after another three peers have spoken) or speaking ratios (e.g., speaking once for every five comments from someone else). Parents and bosses can help the ASD children and employees with similar methods. There is no better way to ruin your relationship with co-workers than delaying the end of the work day.

9. *Interrupting and being the know-it-all.* These are all skills most people learn in elementary school, but they often bear re-learning in a new environment. No one likes to be interrupted. I had one student who, in the three years that I worked with him, never once let me finish a sentence in any of our discussions. Other students miss the point I am trying to make because they are constantly correcting my facts, my wording, my spelling, or pointing out and laughing about times I use wrong words, verb tense, or pronouns. For some ASD teens, this is a habit. They have trained themselves to focus on the pieces of the discussion at the expense of the point. Parents likely do not notice that this is happening because it has been happening for so long and is so much

a part of the cadence of their conversation. Parents should ask their adult friends to honestly tell them if their child is a "know-it-all" or does not let people finish their sentences.

10. *Failing to participate.* This is a more passive version of refusing to follow an instruction (see #4). Some ASD individuals have learned to cope with problems managing the pace and content of conversations, or the relatively harsh sensory experience of group discussions (such as in a classroom) by completely tuning out and daydreaming. Even though focusing, following, and participating in complex and chaotic conversations can be tough, practicing the act of being engaged and resisting the urge to go to your daydream place makes the process easier over time.

CHAPTER 11

PEERS, FRIENDS, AND ENEMIES (LATERAL RELATIONSHIP MANAGEMENT)

Lateral Relationships

Across the hierarchy (or, looking at the people on your same or similar rung) is the other way to relate to others (as opposed to relating vertically, or up and down the hierarchy). These relationships include peers, friends, romantic partners, co-workers, and enemies.

With very few exceptions, the natural tendency of lateral relationships is to move toward an ever-deepening intimacy and stronger bond. The discussion I often have with Autism Spectrum Disorder (ASD) teens is that bonds are about more than just formation (i.e., making friends), they are the process of building and strengthening (i.e., maintaining relationships). I think a lot of people who teach social skills to children on the Spectrum or other individuals interested in making more friends focus almost exclusively on the friendship-making end of things. They teach children how to introduce themselves, come up with conversation topics, and how to be nice and likable. After years of such training I often talk to the exasperated ASD teen who comes to me to say that they have tried and tried but have no friends. I will ask them who they are friendly with, and they can name a couple of other teens. Then I ask them when was the last time they invited a peer to do something social, or even sat with them at lunch, and I get blank stares.

Storage Dynamics

Lateral relationships are always dynamic and always in flux. They are either growing closer or growing more distant, and at various rates, but they are never stagnant. You may be remembering an old school friend that you saw the other day for the first time in a while and it was as if no time had passed. Relationships can act like bank accounts in that we can store up experience, goodwill, feelings, grievances, and have them preserved for a long time. Storing up, however, is an active and dynamic process and often requires some amount of maintenance (e.g., telling stories from your youth about throwing fireworks out of a car window with a friend). Most of the ASD teens I talk with have limited understanding of just how much work goes into maintaining a friendship or a romantic relationship, let alone making it deeper and more meaningful. Some I talk to believe that just because they are being nice they should have friends. As adults we would serve our children well to better describe the process of making and maintaining friendships. The good news is that efforts toward building friendships and romantic relationships (so long as you have chosen a good partner) usually pay dividends.

Enemies

I did an informal survey once of all the social skills classes I taught, and the vast majority of the ASD teens I surveyed could identify an enemy they had. My simple question was, "How many of you feel you have an enemy?" For years I had been listening to children in my office describe these intensely antagonistic relationships. In some cases, they clearly spent more time thinking about and talking about these supposed enemies than they did any other relationship. What was also interesting was how convinced they were that their supposed enemy was out to get them. More often than not I knew the "enemy" personally as it was another student at the school, and knew for certain that the other student did not consider them an antagonist or enemy. In fact, I was nearly certain that most of these "enemies" did not even think about the other person at all.

The question I had in the beginning of my search was whether or not these ASD teens were experiencing clinical levels of paranoia (e.g., "People are out to get me"). I have come to the conclusion that the teens were thinking about their enemies not in a clinically paranoid way, but in a self-referent way. The ASD population struggles with breaking out of the "self at center" thinking that is common among teens. With a typical adolescent, one can ask, "Could it be another way?" (e.g., "Is it possible you think about them more than they think about you?") and the Neurotypical (NT) teen can honestly answer in the affirmative. This action, consciously stepping out of the center and putting someone else there, is a Theory of Mind activity, and challenging for ASD individuals. It is not paranoia, I have come to discover; it is a delay in Theory of Mind development.

Even the enemy relationship requires maintenance. From what I can tell, the ASD teens I questioned about their enemies were able to narrate several interactions they had had in the past with their enemy that proved they were at odds with each other. Several interesting things stuck out in these stories. First, the situations they described were, by and large, ambiguous situations. By that I mean that the intent of the aggravating event, even if it was a direct interaction between the two people, was not clear. For instance, one student told me that his enemy bumps into him in the hall most days, and this was a classic move to aggravate him because he knows he does not like to be touched, and he asked him the year before to not bump into him. When I did some digging, it turned out that the bumping events happened more on the order of occasionally, and almost always between classes when the hallways are packed. And they had neighboring lockers. The bumping was clearly an infrequent and ambiguous event, but the student in my office chose to see it as antagonistic behavior.

The second thing was that the grievances my student had with his "enemy" became a sort of grievance list, and seemed rehearsed. In fact, if I asked him to repeat the events several days later, he would come up with the same events in the same order. It seemed to me that this student had created a list in his mind of evidence that this other student was an enemy. Some events seemed legitimate and worth trying to work out, and some events seemed more ambiguous or accidental. This student then seemed to be rehearsing this list (i.e., maintenance) and getting more and more convinced with each rehearsal that the other student was his enemy.

I shared with my classes after the survey what I thought constituted an enemy (someone who is actively out to get you) and told them enemies are a rare relationship and did not think any of the relationships they described were enemies. Next, when I had a student in my office on this issue I refused to let them rehearse their grievance list. They would tell me the events, I would dismiss some as ambiguous and offer to help them work out others, but if I discovered that they were not interested in resolving any of these situations, I would state they could never talk about these events again to me (unless they were interested in resolving the events). I would also coach their parents to do the same: refuse to listen to them rehearse their list out loud. Interestingly, stopping the rehearsal of the list preceded a decrease in feelings that this person was an enemy and antagonist.

Ideal Friend

Most times when I ask parents what practical things they would like for their ASD child, they respond with one of two things: friends, or more friends. Parents really want their children to appreciate and enjoy about their childhood what they enjoyed, and most of us can look back fondly at our friends and the experiences we had together.

Most ASD children know that society (or, at least, their parents) thinks having friends is a good thing. Most people believe that next to quality (best friends), quantity is the best thing to look for in friendships. More friends usually means the person is more well-liked, more popular, has a more positive reputation, has more people that will stand up for him or her in a fight, more offers for rides to school, and more romantic partners. The reality is that we seem to be pre-programed for a limited number of friends. This relates to the finite nature of relationships: a person with more friends tends to have less potential for deep relationships than a person with fewer friends. Remember our initial premise that says friendships require work and investment. We are all limited in the amount of time and energy we have in our lives. Some people choose to spend more of it on relationships (and less on video games, for instance) than others, but there is a limit we all reach.

Most ASD teens know that the correct answer is to say that they want more friends. Many of them who say it would also pass a polygraph in saying they really would like more friends. The reality, however, is that there is a disconnect between wanting something and the effort it takes to get it. When I have explored this goal of more friends with ASD teens, more often than not what they are saying is they would like closer or better friends. And when we get down to it, they admit that they really just want one good friend—someone they can pour themselves into and who can pour themselves into them.

I really have seen the range in preference for friendships. There are people, I do believe, who can be perfectly content with little or no social contact. Some ASD teens I have met are content to interact exclusively with their parents and a sibling. What I tell parents who are worried about the relatively little socializing their child does, and their child's seemingly low drive to socialize, is that humans are relational beings and it is really part of good overall well-being to have a social network. The need for social contact is part of our DNA, and even the most isolated individual needs to go into town every so often for supplies. People really do not do well when they have no social contact, so yes, parents, I agree that your child should socialize. However, I caution you about making decisions about how to socialize.

As a case in point, I have met several very quiet and reserved ASD teens who have told me they are looking for a best friend. My one desire is to make a way for them to have this friend. We talk about where teens hang out, what they do, what they talk about, and generally work on ways to increase the chances of a good first interaction and future interactions. I became terribly frustrated when I saw these teens pass up, time after time, great opportunities for socializing, hanging out, dates, or any number of invitations and opportunities that would likely lead to the deepening of a relationship. Finally, I set aside some time with one of these teens and asked what, exactly, would convince them to spend the time to get to know someone better. Together we created a list of characteristics and circumstances and I discovered that this ASD teen wanted someone with the exact same interests, the same demeanor, the same opinions and outlooks on life, and someone who was okay with as little or as much contact as they dictated at any particular time (e.g., not too pushy, but texts when wanted). This student was looking for the perfect friend under the perfect circumstances. I explained that this was not only unreasonable, but actually impossible since his friend would possess the same apparent level of apathy he has, and thus they would never find each other. His response was stunning to me in that he was totally okay with waiting for this fictitious and highly unlikely relationship to happen. He wanted a close friend exactly like himself, and was generally unwilling to compromise. He was content to wait.

What I really want to pass along to you, the parent and Native Expert, is that outside some social contact for well-being, friendship needs and needs for affiliation and connection seem to be an individual difference. By this I mean that each person's social needs and preferences are unique, and seem to be based on a number of different factors. Parents should be very careful about imposing their values about relationships on their ASD child. This has been one of the more frequent areas of discontent I have seen in parents and ASD teens. Parents believe that their child should have more friends and work harder at friendships. ASD teens know this is an expectation and thus want more friends almost exclusively because their parents say it is the right thing to do. They seem unable to fulfill expectations because the drive is not to affiliate and associate (a core drive of making and maintaining friendships), but a drive to please their parents.

How to Support Your Child in Building Friendships

- Ask your child what they are looking for in a friend, and discuss this without going into task-mode (e.g., "Okay, let's go get you some friends!").

- Make sure they have the basic skills to make (and maintain) a friend (ask a therapist if you have questions).

- Realize that making friends is actually a very complex social process. Feel free to break down the task and help out in parts.

- Provide them with the opportunity to make friends (i.e., insist they use some of their free time outside their room).

- Recognize the potential value of online friendships (see the section below on internet-based relationships).

- Make sure your child knows some of the basic tenets of friendships (e.g., reciprocity, loyalty, compromise).

- See your own beliefs about friends (quality and quantity) as opinions and not facts.

- Make sure they are not avoiding socializing because of anxiety (social anxiety is very common in the ASD population; ask a therapist if you have questions).

- Apply the five-year developmental delay rule when looking at the quality of friendships as well as who your child chooses to befriend and how they interact.

What ASD Teens Bring to a Friendship

If your child is motivated to make a friend, or wants to foster a current peer or friend relationship into something deeper in which he or she can invest, there are some things you need to know about your child. In my experience, there are fewer groups of people who are more genuine, honest, accepting, loyal, and interesting than the ASD population.

Why has this group of teens who have traditionally had it so hard socially developed corporately to be the best friends ever? I think it actually has to do with three factors. First, these children have had a lot of hardship (more than your average child), and more often than not they have had at least one adult by their side (usually a parent) supporting them unconditionally. I cannot tell you how important it is to have another person's unconditional support while going through tough times. Without such support people can become bitter. With appropriate support they have the chance to build character and to become better people.

Second, related to the above reason, is the unfortunate consequence of being picked on and teased. Persevering through situations where they were victims of subtle and overt social and academic discrimination over the years has made many ASD individuals adamant about overcoming discrimination. Every single time I have had an ASD teen in my office for being mean to another child I only have to remind them that someone was mean to them in the past and now they are passing that meanness and discrimination on to another person. This activates in them an inescapable sense of empathy and regret, and it is all it takes to get them to apologize and become that person's advocate. With the help of the parent, the ASD child can emerge as an advocate for the little guy; someone of whom you should be proud.

The third reason these teens make great friends is that most ASD teens I have met have no idea what I mean when I talk about "the games people play." The notion of consciously manipulating someone for your own personal gain just does not occur to these teens. This is why, despite their strange body language and facial expressions, ASD teens are terrible liars. There seems to be little drive to deceive or manipulate others. It is as if they are untouched by the worst mankind has to offer. This does not mean that they are not selfish. It simply means that rarely do I find an ASD teen who will willingly make someone suffer so they can get something they want.

CHAPTER 12

SOCIAL MEDIA AND TEXT–BASED COMMUNICATION

The Internet is Here

When I first started working in Mental Health, one question parents would often ask is, "Should I let my child be on the internet?" I would discuss this issue quite a bit with parents and we would come up with an answer that was both professionally sound and fit the values of the family. Usually it was some compromise that included a lot of "yes, but"-type statements. Yes, they can be on the internet, but only in a shared space in the house. Yes, they can be on the internet, but only at school, and so on.

It occurred to me one day as I was talking with a group of professionals about this issue that the parents and I were pursuing the wrong question. The actual question was to ask under what conditions Autism Spectrum Disorder (ASD) teens should be on the internet. The internet, like it or not, is here. There is no escaping it. Your children, and all those children who were born after the early 1990s, have really never experienced a life without the internet. The internet is no longer a luxury in Western society. The internet is vital to staying informed and being able to access resources needed to stay a contributing member of society today.

Your child is on the internet, so you need to address it. If your child is not on the internet, he or she should be. The internet is now the main way people interact. Not being on the internet will add to the disadvantages your ASD child faces. I want to be clear that I am not saying the internet is good or bad, it is simply a reality of life at this point. Individuals who decry the internet and shun its use are dwindling in number and voice. I encourage parents to make themselves familiar with the internet if they are not already. This will be helpful in making informed parenting decisions for your child's safety and advantage.

Qualities of the Internet

We all know, or can suspect, some of the risks of the internet. First, everything you do on the internet, including your browsing history, is recorded in some way, shape, or form. People should assume that every keystroke is being recorded and stored indefinitely. Each time society thinks it is starting to get a handle on this concept of privacy and security, some individual, corporation, government, or other entity steps in and shows us just how vulnerable we are to being monitored. In addition, you hear of people losing their job or failing to get a job because of a revealing photo they posted ten years earlier, but forgot about.

There are also people on the internet who either wish your child harm, or consider them collateral damage, or a means to an end. There are predators and other harmful people accessing the same internet as your children, posting content and gathering information. Some of them are even looking for children just like yours. The internet is based on the concept of free and open access, but free access is not a moral code, and it does not initially exclude people who wish your children harm.

Finally, your child knows more about the internet than you do. Maybe you think that because you work for a software or hardware developer, or maybe because you are a web designer or in some area of tech, you therefore know more about the internet than your child. Maybe you have been using the internet for 30 years and know all there is to know about it. The reason I know your child knows more about the internet than you is because the internet is constantly evolving, and it is evolving to meet the needs of your child, and not you. The internet is constantly changing to meet the (supposed) needs and desires of the pre-teen, teen, and young adult demographic. You will be playing catch-up as long as your children are in that demographic.

I am sure parents can come up with more internet risks. You have been managing risks when it comes to your children for a long time now. But the internet is not an inherently bad place, it is just a place. Good things can happen there, too.

Low-context Communication

When I was first using email to communicate with my co-workers, friends, family, bosses, teachers, and others, I quickly discovered all the limitations of the medium. Email is terrible for conveying non-verbal messages such as tone of voice, sarcasm, emphasis, emotion, or other contextually based information. Accidentally hitting the Caps Lock and writing and sending the email to your boss usually got you fired because that was read as a sign you were yelling your response. I WILL NOT BE IN TODAY. I AM SICK (which might read as, "Sick of you and all of your general incompetence as a boss"). People experimented with adding more context to such text-based communication (e.g., emoticons), but we never got anywhere close to a face-to-face interaction as far as true communication is concerned. Several decades later, people still often misread and misinterpret email and text conversations.

It was because of this that I was concerned about ASD children using the internet, and specifically text-based (typing) communication. If I had a hard time with it (and I was the communications expert), how much would they struggle? What actually happened and what I discovered surprised me. Relative to how these ASD teens usually communicate with each other and their teachers and parents, they actually had fewer incidents of social rule-breaking and social failures while communicating over the internet than when they communicated face-to-face. Text-based communication actually seemed easier and more comfortable to them than face-to-face communication.

Text-based communication is the great equalizer in communications. It is what I consider to be one of the more simplistic and basic forms of communication. It is the most straightforward and least nuanced. I remember when I was learning Japanese I found that I did much better on written portions than spoken portions of exams. There were several reasons for this, and I think these reasons apply to ASD teens using text-based communications as well:

- Writing (like the experience one gets with composing texts) allows one to artificially control the speed of input and output. You do not really have to tell your conversation partner to repeat something when it is written. It is right there, you can just read it again. You can also take your time composing and getting your response just right if you choose.

- Even the best writers know that much of their audience will not be able to hear the sarcasm, emphasis, incredulity, or happiness in the voice of their characters, unless they specifically say it is there (e.g., "He replied, incredulously, 'I asked for a Coke. This is a Pepsi...'"). This whole part of the conversation that ASD teens struggle to interpret in face-to-face discussions (called pragmatic language) is simply not present, or present in very small doses, in text-based communication. It is not available to anyone, so the playing field has been essentially leveled in communication.

- I alluded to this above, but ASD individuals often report struggling with the speed of conversations. Much of this is due to slower processing speed (time it takes to receive and interpret the input, and compose and utter the response), and some ASD teens tell me they cannot keep up with much of the peer conversation that is going on around them, especially if it is about a topic with which they are not familiar. Text-based communication is all about turn-taking: you type, now I type, now you type, and so on. This very deliberate turn-taking again slows things down and allows one to be a more active participant.

- The internet is economical. People used to have to pay for international calls, then pay for long-distance calls, then pay for roaming charges, and then pay for separate services that allowed us to make all those calls more cheaply. If I did not want to call people, then I actually had to go to where they were. I had to leave the house, and that involved getting a ride, catching a bus, or paying for fuel. The internet has effectively done away with the cost of communication as it relates to actual money, time, and skill.

Not only is text-based and other internet-mediated communication making communicating and socializing easier for many ASD individuals because of the low-context communication, it also means they do not have to leave their house if they do not want to. Using the internet to communicate is, in many respects, a better match for ASD teens, and one I encourage parents to take advantage of.

Parameters of Social Media

Every parent needs to be armed with a good set of rules and expectations when it comes to managing social media and internet use. Regardless of what choices you make, you should make your rules do-able and realistic, clear, reasonable, and systematically and predictably flexible.

Do-able and Realistic

Initially, you are going to have to monitor compliance, which means you need to set rules that you can actually monitor. Do not set rules that need to be followed when the child is in his or her room with the door shut, or when you are asleep. Also, be careful about setting up rewards and consequences for compliance that make your life harder. This is a general guideline about rule-making that actually applies to all rules and boundaries you set in the house—not just those for the internet.

Clear

This should go without saying, but avoid vague terms and concepts. The more specific you can be, the better. Clarifying expectations is actually a process your children may resist at the beginning. Instead of saying "for a little while" (when referring to how long they can be on a social media site), say a specific number ("30 minutes"). There is an inverse correlation between your level of clarity and the number of arguments you will have about the rules.

Reasonable

Fifteen minutes of video game playing a day is unreasonably short. Fifteen hours is unreasonably long. "Reasonable" is based more on values and experiences, and the Native Expert is the best person to decide what is reasonable for the child. Feel free to use the discussion about what is reasonable as a time to bargain or compromise with your child. Not everything needs to be debated, though. Many of the things you think of as privileges your children see as rights, or things they deserve.

Systematically and Predictably Flexible

The standards children have for how they use their time and their resources should change as they get older and become more disciplined and experienced. The most significant change is that responsibility for monitoring should always be shifting toward the child. I have seen too many parents resign themselves to monitoring and being the conscience of their child indefinitely. Children should be able to predict accurately when they are following the rules, and when they are not. They should be able to predict rewards and consequences. They should be allowed to choose their level of independence based exclusively on their actions (and not the mood or memory of the parent). If the rules you set up have no end point or conclusion that your child can tell me (the professional) about when I ask, then that is a good place to start working.

My Internet Rules

- Every parent should have unlimited access to their ASD child's internet and text-based activity all the time. This means that parents should have all of their child's login names and passwords. You should have unlimited and spontaneous access to their personal computer and phone. Most parents believe strongly that their child should have some privacy, and especially as they get older. I am not a big fan of privacy between children and their parents. The main reason is that children are inexperienced and make uninformed decisions, and the chances of bad decisions increase with their level of privacy. Children need help in not making bad decisions, hurting others, and embarrassing themselves and their parents. How does the child who wants it get more privacy?

By proving they can handle it. Privacy in the house is not a right, it is absolutely earned.

- Parents should do their children a favor and reduce the number of temptations they have to make bad decisions. You will need to see what is tempting for your child. Can they resist being on the computer until 2am on a school night? If not, do them a favor and take their computer away from them at 8pm. Does your child have a "friend" on the internet who makes them feel bad about themselves every time they interact? Do your child a favor and block that friend. Better yet, call the friend's parents and talk to them about what is happening. Work something out with the friend and their parents so the children can interact and be less likely to fight. There are so many things out there your child has to negotiate and make decisions about. I think it is okay to help them by removing some of the temptations.

- Monitor your child for obsessive internet-based behaviors. Some children write Fan-fiction (using a pre-existing character like Luke Skywalker and telling an alternate or additional storyline that they make up), and write it obsessively. Writing Fan-fiction can easily become an addiction for some ASD teens and a way to avoid actual social interactions. Some ASD teens are addicted to pornography and cannot stop looking at it even while at school. Some ASD teens are addicted to gaming, or modifying their computers, or checking social media sites, or checking the weather or stocks, or any other interest that has become an obsession. Parents can test the level of obsession by restricting their child's access to computers, phones, and the internet. Can they stop thinking about it when they do not have access? If there does appear to be an addictive quality to your child's internet use, you should consult a professional for assistance.

- Teach your children that social responsibility extends to behavior on the internet. The distance between people interacting on the internet (both in mileage and time) sometimes allows us to drop or suspend our inhibitions and say and do things we will regret later. Parents should research online resources such as "commonsensemedia.org" and search "internet etiquette" for ideas about how to work with children on this issue.

- Have your child observe the same sets of greetings online as they do (or should do) in person. Social behavior on social media is very much a free-for-all. Have your children say hello and goodbye and thank you whenever appropriate. Signing off of chats is especially important.

- "Trolling" has become a popular way to interact on the internet. Trolling is the act of intentionally antagonizing people in order to get a desired negative reaction from them (often called a "rant"). For instance, I have heard of people "trolling" cancer support groups on the internet. Individuals will log on to the support group under the guise of a person with cancer and then, once active in the group, say hurtful things to the other members of the group in order to get a critical, offended response. The bad news is that your child might think trolling is funny. ASD children especially have a hard time understanding what is so wrong with the act of trolling. I hear a lot of "I wasn't serious" or "I was just kidding" excuses from students who troll on the internet.

- Go over with your child conversations and other interactions they have had on the internet. Look at what they post and talk about it with them. Your child should learn to use the internet appropriately not because of a fear of retribution or losing their privilege, but out of an understanding of how it works to meet their needs and the needs of those around them. One technique I use is to have ASD teens print out conversations and go through them line by line with me. Parents should give their children a strong foundation for a lifetime of internet use.

• Some ASD teens cannot handle unlimited access to the internet and computers. As much as I would like all ASD teens to graduate from school and be completely independent adults, making great decisions for themselves, I know that some of them will always need to have restricted access to the internet or computers. I have had some clients, when living alone, choose not to have the internet in their home. Some limit themselves to a phone that only makes telephone calls. The important point is that these individuals came to these conclusions themselves based on thoughtful reflection of what they know they can and cannot handle.

PART IV

PARENTS AND PROFESSIONALS

CHAPTER 13

MENTAL HEALTH

In the same way that our understanding of the causes of Spectrum disorders has evolved slowly over time, our understanding of appropriate treatments and interventions has also evolved. More recently, mental health professionals have begun to effectively differentiate symptomatology that is the result of the neurological condition of the Spectrum disorder from that which is the result of a mental illness (e.g., Clinical Depression), and to consider how the Spectrum disorder and the mental illness might interact.

A Spectrum disorder, at this point and time, is life-long. Parents do well to accept that their Autism Spectrum Disorder (ASD) child is going to struggle with issues of social and pragmatic language skills, Executive Functioning (EF) skills, and Sensory Integration problems on some level for the rest of their lives. In this book, I have offered ideas on how to mediate some of these disabilities and reduce their overall effect on your child's day-to-day functioning, but these problems are not going away. Symptomatology such as isolation, social avoidance, low energy and other things, on the other hand, absolutely can be treated separately and have a different prognosis.

What parents need is to find at least one professional who can tell the difference between a behavior that is the function of the Spectrum diagnosis, and one that is the function of some other mental health issue. For instance, some ASD individuals will always avoid big gatherings of people because they are sound-sensitive. They can wear earplugs, but the sound sensitivity is likely a function of their Spectrum diagnosis and will be with them for life—something they need to learn to manage. Some ASD individuals avoid large gatherings, however, because the thought of having to socialize with new people makes them anxious. Indeed, they have been avoiding such gatherings all of their lives and as teenagers they feel anxious just at the mention of Senior Prom. This type of anxiety is usually treatable and something your teen can work through. He does not have to accept that he will feel anxious about meeting new people for the rest of his life.

Finding a Competent Professional

Specialized training to work clinically with ASD individuals is becoming more popular, but few professionals to date have received this training. On the flip side, nearly every mental health professional you meet has been trained to deal with depressed adults. Working with adults with depression is considered a general area of study in mental health training; however, working with the ASD population is, at this time, still very specialized. It will not always be this way, but for the time being it is. Having experience is different, too, from having training. Anyone can attend a workshop and learn about how to work with ASD individuals, but there is no population I know of that is as challenging to work with clinically than the ASD population.

For this reason, I encourage parents to choose your ASD child's therapist or direct-care professional very carefully. When I consult with parents on this issue, I usually try to give them this advice:

- Act like a consumer. Ask the potential therapist what their experience is in working with this population. A lot of experience is not, however, always necessary. Some clinicians have a lot of experience but very little drive. Some have little experience but very high intelligence and drive. Understanding of the basics of working with this population, minus extensive experience, plus a lot of energy and good clinical acumen can be a very good thing. Your therapist needs to be ready to hustle (i.e., combine exertion and intelligence in their work). Ask your potential therapist these questions:

  - What is your experience working with the ASD population?

  - What sorts of treatment strategies do you use with this population (what do you find effective)?

○ How involved can we, as parents (i.e., Native Experts), be in therapy?

○ How often will you need to see my child? (*Note:* weekly for at least a couple of months is what it takes for most therapists to become a useful resource.)

○ What are reasonable therapeutic goals for this population?

○ Would you be able to provide recommendations for other professionals, such as psychiatrists, educational therapists, or mentors that specialize in working with this population?

- Ask the therapist to specifically describe their treatment of choice for the Spectrum population. The popular therapy right now is Cognitive Behavioral Therapy (CBT). CBT is popular for several reasons. It is the most thoroughly researched therapy, and one of the most common therapies taught in clinical training programs. It is also effective in treating a range of mental health problems. For these reasons, CBT is the treatment style therapists are likely to say they use when you ask. I use CBT in my general practice, but not with ASD teens. Positive results in CBT rely heavily on the effective use of introspection, being able to describe your experience to the therapist, reciprocal communication, and quickly building a strong bond with the therapist. All of these processes are, in my experience, challenging for ASD individuals to do without specific training and extensive practice.

- My treatments of choice are Behavioral Therapy and Systems Therapy (or some form of Family Therapy). Ask the therapist if they have training in these therapies, or ones like them, and if they feel comfortable using them. I prefer using Behavioral Therapy for therapy with both ASD and Neurotypical (NT) individuals because a person does not have to know why something works before benefiting from it. Insight and meaning (major ingredients in therapies such as CBT and Existential Therapy) are exciting and motivating, and often the result of a successful behavioral intervention and guided reflection. I sometimes use Systems Therapy because only one motivated family member (usually one of the parents) is necessary to make meaningful change in the family. Both of these therapies have the downside of needing little to no buy-in from the client to work. This is a downside because even when something is working and change is happening, most parents want their child to be happy about it and committed to the process of therapy. If parents can let that prerequisite go, these therapies can be very effective.

- Ask the therapist if they would ever be willing to see your child outside the office. How flexible are they with the "therapy hour"? In nearly every case I have worked with in my practice, my client has identified a treatment goal that means we will need to meet in some setting outside my office. Some people have problems with large crowds, so we have to go to the mall. Some have problems with public transportation, so we have to ride the bus together. Some have problems with their boss and their boss and my client agree to meet me in the boss's office before work. All of these scenarios can make a therapist nervous because they all pose threats to confidentiality and thus increase liability. Your therapist, however, needs to know how to manage that liability and be willing to accommodate for the purpose of providing the best care possible to your child.

- As mentioned above, your child's therapist needs to have an extensive referral base. It is likely that there will be issues that come up in the course of care that your therapist cannot manage directly, but will or should know someone who can manage them. For instance, most of my clients are also prescribed medication. Many of my clients need some sort of educational or tutoring support. Some of my clients have other physical health issues. I cannot do direct care for these issues, but I know people who can, and I know that these people have experience either working with ASD individuals, or know when to call me when they need consultation.

- Much of my work with the ASD population can look more like what a social worker might do, and less like what a traditional psychotherapist would do (e.g., the couch, talk about whatever you want to talk about). I spend a lot of time with my clients planning things, making lists, and helping them make phone calls. Outside therapy I respond to parent questions and talk with other professionals who are also providing direct care to my client. I consider myself the ringleader of the operation, and your child's therapist needs to be ready to take on that responsibility. Does the therapist return your calls promptly? Does the provider sound like they know what they are doing? Do they have a treatment plan they can describe to you in a couple of minutes? Some therapists pride themselves on being a non-directive blank slate (there is nothing wrong with this) where the client can take the therapy hour talking about whatever they want to talk about. Your child probably needs someone who is organized, more directive, and is not afraid to give you and your child advice and be authoritative.

Therapy Options
Below are some of the more common therapeutic options you will have for dealing with your child's mental health and social issues.

Individual Therapy
This is much of what I described above when looking for a therapist. Individual therapy for the ASD population looks a little more like working with a social worker, and less like working with Sigmund Freud. Individual therapy needs to be goal-oriented, largely directive (i.e., the therapist almost always has an agenda for the hour), and transparent (i.e., the parent knows or should be able to know how the therapist and child are spending their time). There should also be some outcomes or changes the therapist can point to in order to discuss progress with the child and the parent. If you cannot tell if your child is doing better after a brief talk with the therapist where you ask how things are progressing, consider warning your therapist that you might take your business elsewhere.

I have several warnings for the parent and Native Experts when looking at individual therapy. First, make sure your child's therapist can work effectively with the other professionals in your child's life, and especially the school teacher. Your child's teacher spends much more time with your child than the therapist, so the therapist needs to be able to work effectively with the teacher. Second, there is a thing called "marking time" that therapists do while waiting for an opportunity to respond to a crisis or teach a new coping strategy or skill. Therapists use this time to build rapport, do assessment, and generally expand the client's comfort level with them and expand their own understanding of the client. Often this can look like the therapist is getting paid to play Connect Four with your child, but it can be a very productive time as well. Crises are often the catalyst for change, and parents need to have a therapist available and informed when the crisis happens. Crises are also not always preventable, so it is quite realistic, in the mental health profession, to be waiting for one and expecting it to happen eventually. What parents need to be careful of is a therapist who is marking time *while* a crisis is happening. Have you ever had a hard time reaching your child's therapist when there is a crisis (where you waited more than 24 hours)? Do you feel like they are not taking the child's problems as seriously as you think they should? Your child's therapist needs to know how to manage the waxing and waning of an ASD individual's life.

Finally, I want to talk a little bit about social skills training in individual therapy. I do not recommend social skills training to be the major goal of therapy. You should be suspicious of a therapist who spends a lot of one-on-one time working exclusively on social skills. There are a couple of reasons for this. First, after the age of 5, most people do not learn many social skills from adults, and certainly not from therapists. People learn and perfect the vast amount of their social skills from their peers. What the therapist needs to be working on is building a basic repertoire of skills that will facilitate peer interaction. Therapists should always be moving toward getting your child around and interacting with their peers if building social skills is the focus of therapy. Second, ASD individuals, especially in childhood and adolescence, struggle with generalization of skills. Generalization is an Executive Functioning activity that allows a person to take things learned in one context and perform them in another. Learning social skills in therapy means your child will get good at socializing with therapists, and that is about it.

How Long Should Individual Therapy Take?

The question of how long therapy should take is one that consumers need to ask. There are therapy models called Brief Therapy that are designed to run for about eight to 12 sessions. Successful Brief Therapy encounters are done with individuals with very discrete issues (panic disorder, job change, low mood, etc.) who are highly motivated and self-directed. Spectrum disorders do not fall into this category, and most teens I work with are not self-directed, even if they seem to be highly motivated. Much of my work with ASD individuals becomes long-term therapy because the issues addressed are more global and include things such as school success and social success. Appropriately involved and engaged parents who follow the instructions of the competent therapist can reduce the overall number of sessions, but I would recommend making the therapist bill a part of your monthly budget.

Part of the reason therapy takes so long is that therapy is an interpersonal process and is highly dependent on the relationship between the therapist and the client. This relationship is called the Therapeutic Alliance. The Therapeutic Alliance (i.e., client's sense of trust, warmth and acceptance from the therapist, therapist's responsiveness to the client's needs) is usually the most important factor in positive therapy outcomes. Building a strong alliance with a client is the first goal of psychotherapy, and I have found that building a strong alliance with an ASD individual can take at least twice as long as with an average NT client. Part of this has to do with the fact that just about every ASD individual I have met has their own, personal non-verbal language (e.g., ways they demonstrate a sense of confusion with their body). Non-verbals are important for the effective communication between the therapist and client. Because of how unique the non-verbal language is of each ASD individual I work with, it is like learning a new language every time I meet a new ASD client. For the ASD client, almost all of our bonding initially is done verbally. I cannot reliably use any non-verbal communication to build my alliance in the beginning of therapy. The reason learning non-verbal cues is a good thing is because it is an incredibly efficient way of communicating. Without that communication source, the process takes a long time.

Group Therapy

Group therapy can be a good place for your child to begin to build a peer group. The reason parents put their ASD child in group therapy with a trained professional and don't just plunk them down in the lunchroom to learn social skills is that the trained professionals can teach not just the social skills and provide for a safe place to practice those skills, but also the therapist can train children in the art of the feedback loop.

When children do something strange or offensive in a social interaction, they usually let each other know. This usually comes in the form of teasing. If a child does not quickly make an adjustment in their behavior, the peer group can move on to tormenting or isolating the child. Prior to tormenting or isolating, teasing is a way peers give each other feedback that the behavior was strange or needs to be done differently. Hundreds and hundreds of social exchanges lead to many micro-adjustments and lessons in socializing, and, over time, people get better at socializing with a wide range of individuals by participating in this feedback loop.

ASD individuals struggle with spontaneously participating in the feedback loop. They struggle with giving feedback to others in ways that are useful, and they struggle with interpreting feedback and incorporating it into their social lexicon. A therapist in a group therapy setting can facilitate this feedback process and teach the children to both give meaningful feedback to their peers, and incorporate feedback that they are receiving from others for the purpose of making social adjustments. I have seen ASD children, once they learn the process and get a sense of the cadence of it, start to use the feedback loop without prompting. It requires a lot of conscious effort and repetition on the part of a good therapist, though. Group therapy is an ideal place to learn some basic social skills in both making and maintaining friendships, initiating and maintaining conversations, and relating across, up, and down the social hierarchy.

Coaching

For children and adults on the Spectrum, coaches can be useful for specialized skills. For instance, if you would like your ASD teen to get a part-time job, you might consider hiring a coach to help them with filling out the application, doing the job interview, figuring out how to use public transportation to get to the job, being on time the first day, and learning the basic skills of the job, among other things. Coaches are effective for other activities such as learning about public transportation, international travel, coming home from residential treatment and reintegrating into the family of origin, and the like. Be very careful to hire a coach who has either experience, or intelligence and drive. Coaches must have insight, a record of practical experience, and intelligence.

Primary Care

A brief note I will make about primary care is that most ASD individuals are intelligent, have access to the internet, and know how to memorize a list of symptoms. This is not exclusive to the ASD population, but more than once I have heard a story of an ASD teen who decided that he had an illness and then successfully convinced a physician to treat that illness. Advice I give to parents is that it is okay to ask to speak to the physician before your child does if you are concerned that they are going to try to convince the physician they have an illness you do not think they have. Give the physician the heads-up and then let them do their job. Also, second opinions are often useful.

Psychiatry and Medication Management

Remember that many of the diagnostic tools your child's psychiatrist uses to determine whether or not they would benefit from certain medications rely on self-report and effectively describing one's internal experience. Your ASD child likely struggles with this level of social communication. Until we get better at using biomarkers for making diagnoses and formulating treatment strategies, we remain dependent on what our clients tell us for forming treatment opinions. The psychiatrists I know that do well in their practice take both the parent and the child seriously, and then call other professionals that work with the child (e.g., therapist, teachers) for verification and consultation.

I am a firm believer in "better living through chemistry." I do know that some people are prescribed medication who do not technically need it, or could manage fine without it. In my experience, though, life is hard enough for ASD individuals and others with developmental and neurological disabilities. If medication can promote well-being and successful coping, that sounds like a positive thing to me. Be sure to call your child's provider with any concerns, and be sure to find a psychiatrist you think is responsive and dependable. Actively work with the psychiatrist to make treatment decisions that make sense for your child and your family.

The Big Three

There are many things parents and their children can do at home with minimal professional support to promote well-being. I am always happy to recommend to the average ASD individual to work on the Big Three: Sleep, Diet, and Exercise.

Sleep

Is your child getting enough sleep each and every night? Children and adolescents need between eight and nine hours of sleep every night. Adults need about seven to eight hours. Your child should go to bed around the same time and wake up around the same time each day, and even on weekends.

Are they getting too little sleep? Are they getting too much sleep? Both too little and too much sleep can negatively affect mood and energy level, among other things. In my experience, ASD individuals report a significant amount of sleep disturbance relative to the general population. Ask your child how long it takes them to fall asleep and how much they are awake at night. Does your child require multiple reminders to wake up in the morning? Would they miss the bus if you did not drag them out of bed? Sleep problems and problems waking up are a great reason to find a qualified therapist. Managing sleep and setting the sleep cycle right in a sustainable way can have a positive effect on many areas of daily living.

Diet

Your ASD child probably has, or had, a restricted diet. It is probably a struggle to get them to eat a balanced meal daily, let alone three times a day. The fact is that your diet, including how much and what you eat, has everything to do with how you feel and how you function. Some ASD children eat too much, and of a very restricted type of food. Some eat too little, and their low energy, lack of focus, and irritability in the afternoon are related to running out of energy. Getting your child to diversify his or her diet and eat an appropriate amount of food from what is available (i.e., what you are making for the rest of the family) can be a challenge. Mealtimes are also one of the best times for families to socialize. Help setting up good eating and mealtime habits is a great reason to see a therapist.

Exercise

Many people do not enjoy exercise, but when is the last time your child played basketball outside, all afternoon, with his or her friends? What is the ratio of time they spend doing sedentary activities such as playing video games, watching TV, and reading relative to activities that involve movement? All teens need about an hour of physical activity a day. How close is your child to meeting that minimum? I have heard a long list of excuses from both ASD teens and their parents about why they cannot exercise or get enough daily movement. Low muscle tone, low stamina, bad experiences in PE class, dislike of competition, and lack of coordination are some of the more common excuses I hear. Most ASD teens will tell me they will not exercise because they do not want to, and no one is forcing them to do so. None of these excuses change the fact that your child is a teenager and needs to move his or her body for about an hour a day. Exercise is also a wonder drug. Exercise can enhance and stabilize mood, improve appetite, decrease irritability, improve quality of sleep, and generally enhance overall well-being. People who exercise regularly feel better than those that do not. Help developing an exercise or activity routine is a great reason to see a therapist.

Anxiety and Depression

As I mentioned above, the most common way psychologists and other mental health professionals identify and treat anxiety and depression is by talking with the client about his or her experience. I usually ask clients a series of open-ended questions (questions that cannot be answered with a "yes" or "no") to make my diagnosis. This can be a problem for ASD individuals because describing one's internal experience to others in a way they can understand is a complex pragmatic language activity. First, you must know what you are feeling physically, cognitively, and emotionally (not an ASD strength). Then, you have to put that information into words that are common parlance (not an ASD strength). Finally, people have to be able to compare their experience to another person's or a standard experience, often using metaphor (e.g., "Does it feel like your head is a volcano?"). Successful use of metaphor is, again, not a strength of most ASD individuals. Diagnosis and treatment relies heavily on interpersonal, verbal interactions with increasingly nuanced descriptions of a largely unobservable state (moods and feelings). Below is how I approach this task with ASD individuals.

Anxiety

A couple of years ago the school where I teach did a voluntary clinical survey of its students about anxiety disorders. The surveyors found that about half the students surveyed qualified for an anxiety disorder. In the years since that survey, my observations with many ASD students and clients over the years has supported this initial finding. Anxiety disorders are rampant in the ASD population.

ASD individuals can suffer the range of anxiety disorders, from low-intensity daily worries (worried all the time, about a lot of different things) to very specific and intense worries and fears, to recurring panic attacks that seem to come out of nowhere, and the like. Obsessive Compulsive Disorder (OCD, an anxiety disorder) seems to be very well-represented in the ASD population as well.

There are several challenges this presents for the therapist. First, it can be difficult to tell the difference between anxious avoiding (I stay in my room because I am afraid to socialize) and lack of interest (I stay in my room because where else would I go?). As previously stated, social anxiety can be treated, but lack of interest has more to do with values and would not likely be something a therapist would address. Second, most ASD children I work with have been experiencing clinical levels of anxiety most of their lives. Anxiety is normal to them, so describing it is like describing the air that you breathe. Finally, anxiety disorders can have a major negative impact on the body. Anxiety can affect a person's ability to get restful sleep, cause appetite disturbance, wear down the body and the body's immune response (so anxiety sufferers can get sick more often), and cause general levels of discomfort to the sufferer. Anxiety, as you may know, also leads to irritability, poor focus and attention, low work performance, and low mood.

If you have concerns about anxiety for your child, I would highly recommend a professional evaluation. Psychologists with experience working with ASD individuals are the best place to look for help, but your child's general practitioner (family doctor) is also a good place to check in.

Consequently, anxiety disorders are relatively straightforward for the qualified professional to treat. I absolutely do not recommend traditional therapeutic interventions (especially CBT) for treating anxiety disorders in ASD individuals. I have seen this backfire more than once. The reasons for this are complex and I cannot go into them here. Behavioral therapies and specific skills training seem to work best for treatment of anxiety disorders. I will warn the parent, though, that I have met more than one ASD individual who requires medication to manage anxiety before the talk-style therapies could make a positive difference to the symptoms. Also, I suspect there are people who need medication long-term to manage their anxiety.

Depression

Most people you meet can discern the difference between the way a clinician uses the word "depression" and the way the rest of society uses it. This ability assumes you know how to both assess your own internal emotional experience and report it to others in a way that makes sense to them. Again, this ability to self-assess and report out is not a strength of the average ASD individual. Most practitioners I know who treat depression rely heavily on self-report for their evaluations. The problem I was having in my own practice with self-reports of depression symptoms from ASD individuals is that reporting symptoms in a flat, emotionless tone is both a sign of the level of depression a person is feeling, and the way most ASD individuals describe their internal experience (depressed or not). When most ASD individuals report on their mood, they sound negative and depressed to me most of the time. I was having a very hard time picking out the ASD-style of realistic "life stinks and then you die" reports from the depressed reports.

My Behaviorist background became useful again when I started incorporating the self-report with reports of the physiological aspects of depression. Depression expresses itself fairly loudly through the body and action (or, in this case, inaction). Depressed people have sleep changes, appetite changes, changes in energy level, changes in self-care, changes in disposition and affect, and the like. The key was to look for the change in these physiological markers.

Low energy, lethargy, bad appetite and sleep, you say? Most parents report to me that "this is my child, exactly" when I tell them what I am looking for. And what I reply to them is that I am looking for whether or not there has been a *change* in these markers. I usually look for changes in the past two weeks and move backward in time from there.

REALISM VS. DEPRESSION

Scientists (e.g., Alloy and Abramson 1979) suggest that we may use a healthy dose of ignorance to preserve a positive outlook on life. In other words, people who are depressed tend to report what is going on around them more accurately than those who are not depressed. Life is hard, life is a struggle, and there is a lot of pain in the world, and we have all developed some ways to protect ourselves from these realities. When ASD individuals talk about how they are doing, or current events, it can often sound tragic or have a heavy focus on negative aspects. This does not always mean these individuals are depressed. Often, it can mean that they are not limited by social convention. We all know that when someone asks you how you are doing, you are supposed to say, "Good, and you?" It is a social rule. More often than not you will get a straight answer from an ASD individual when asking this question. Either they do not know the rule, or do not care (usually the latter). The intervention here is teaching your ASD child about the difference between greetings and assessments. I have had more than one discussion with an ASD teen about what adults think when the teen says they are depressed and are thinking about suicide. The students are not thinking about committing suicide, they are just thinking about it the way you are thinking about it now as you are reading this. I tell the child that adults will take the words depression and suicide very seriously when you say them and be concerned for you, and that these words have very strong meaning for school personnel who work with teens.

Agoraphobia vs. Being a Hermit vs. Isolation

Your ASD child may choose a life of relative solitude when he or she grows up and becomes an independent adult. They may be happiest when alone and things are quiet and peaceful. The drive to be alone in this sense is different from agoraphobia (fear of being away from comfortable, predictable places) and the isolation that is symptomatic of depression. One caveat I will mention, however, is that social interaction is a factor that protects people from depression. As mentioned elsewhere, even the hermit must go into town for supplies now and then.

The Depressed Identity

We are all looking for what makes us special and different from all other people. This quest is especially active in adolescence. Some ASD individuals I have met have chosen to identify with their mood disorder, or a mood disorder they think they have. They have learned the lingo and they know what combinations of words will get people to interact with them in a predictable, care-taking way. Children identifying how they feel and seeking out support when they are depressed is a good thing. Children seeking out the same support when they are not depressed can be risky. I strongly encourage parents to beware of habits that solicit necessary support or intervention. I am not saying to ignore your child when they are reporting feeling bad and you think they are faking. What I am saying is that you should have a discussion about the meaning of terms (e.g., depression, suicide, killing, shooting up the place) and what people will assume when they are used. Encourage them to use these heavy terms only when they accurately describe their state, and come up with a couple of individuals (a teacher, parents, a therapist) they can use them with.

Drugs, Alcohol, and Suicide

Research is supporting the notion that ASD individuals use drugs and alcohol and think about suicide as much as NT individuals, in general. You can find a thorough review of recent findings about Autism and suicide by Lynne Soraya (2013a) in a *Psychology Today* blog post. Autismspeaks.org is also a resource for parents of children on the Spectrum to learn more about these issues. Nancy Reagan's "Just Say No" campaign in the 1980s to combat the increasing use of drugs has become something of a joke. It was catchy and we can all remember it, but it was largely ineffective. Telling most teens they cannot or should not do something usually makes them want to do it more. Also, Mrs. Reagan never told children what to do instead of doing drugs. If the campaign was "Just Say No, and Then Go Have a Healthy Snack," it might have worked better. "Just Say No" does have some traction with ASD teens, though. Remember what I said about ASD teens seeking balance and peace? As long as you can make a useful argument (drugs will harm you in this particular way), I think this intervention can be helpful.

ASD teens do use drugs and alcohol, though, and it is important to consider why they do. The stories I have heard about drug and alcohol use and abuse with the ASD population tend to revolve around the idea of fitting in and doing what "normal" teens are doing. I have seen rational, logically thinking ASD teens make bad decisions because they think that is what is expected of a typical teenager, and they want to be thought of as typical, or certainly do not want to stand out negatively from the group. Again, all of this reasoning lends itself to meaningful discussion with your ASD teen. Please have these discussions, and keep the issue of drugs and alcohol on the table. Parents should absolutely plan to discuss the legal age of drinking and illegal drug use.

Just the Facts about Suicide

The absolute most effective way to find out if an ASD teen is contemplating suicide is to ask them. Most people who lie about suicidal intent are afraid of what people will think of them, or are afraid of worrying the person who is asking. These are not concerns for the average ASD teen. If your teen says yes to suicidal ideation (thinking about suicide), ask them if they have a plan for how to kill themselves. Generally speaking, the more plausible and detailed the plan, the greater the risk.

In my experiences with ASD teens and suicide, a surprising number of children I screen report thinking about killing themselves by stabbing themselves. I cannot account for the relatively large number of teens I have talked to who reported this plan. Some of them have told me they admire the Samurai and other groups who perform such ritualistic suicide with a blade when they are disgraced. Perhaps imagining death by honorable and ritualistic stabbing helps them feel better about mistakes they have made, or their shortcomings. All of this is information you can follow up on. Why this method? Why would you want to die? What do you think people would think if you were gone? How do you think our (parents) lives would change if we did not have you?

It goes without saying, though, that any discussion or suspicion of suicide should be taken very seriously. The reality of suicide is that most people, at some time in their lives, have thought about suicide. I am making this statement to say that it is important for you to keep your wits if your child responds in the affirmative to thinking about suicide. Worrying about how they will respond is not a reason to avoid asking them the question. It means you need to be ready with a response if your child states they are thinking or have thought about suicide. Start with, "Do you have a plan, a way you would kill yourself?" and go from there. If you are concerned at any point in the process, seek professional help immediately. This could involve calling your child's therapist or pediatrician, or a suicide hotline. If you feel immediate intervention is required, contact emergency services (911 in the US or 999 in the UK).

CHAPTER 14

TRANSITIONS

One of the most common questions I get, and have been getting for many years, is what happens to Autism Spectrum Disorder (ASD) teens when they graduate from school. When I started working with ASD teens the professional community was, for the first time, answering in the affirmative to the question, "Can individuals on the Spectrum finish school in a traditional setting?" The current focus seems to be on increasing success in the college setting. I suspect the next area of focus will be on how to make ASD individuals successful in the workplace. There are already some pioneering sources out there attempting to answer the question of how the work world can use the incredible talents of this ASD population (see Soraya 2013b; Stanford 2011). Look for much more of this in the near future.

Turning 18

There is nothing magical about turning 18. Developmentally, it is not really even the most important time in one's life. It is, however, the time that society, at least in the West, starts to give individuals certain expectations. Laws go into effect, consequences can increase, privileges are granted, and certain protections are taken away. Culturally, turning 18 is a truly meaningful time. It is the time when children become adults and move out of the house. Individuals can become more functional members of a capitalistic society through having the ability to vote, buy cigarettes, and sign for loans without a parent signature.

Most ASD individuals I meet are not ready to become independent adults at age 18. Part of that has to do with the disability and developmental delay, and part of that is cultural, as we seem to be slowing down the process of independence for everyone.

Young adults are living at home longer, getting married and having children later, and becoming financially independent at a slower rate than they used to. There are many reasons for this cultural shift, but my major advice to parents who are desperate to meet this age 18 deadline is "slow down." Unless there is some pressing need, there is no reason to expect that your ASD child is going to turn 18 and suddenly be able to do everything independently.

An issue I sometimes process in therapy with families of ASD soon-to-be 18-year-olds is the parent who says, "I moved out of the house at 17 and a half and I have not been back since," or some form of that sentiment. My message to parents is that not only is that expectation probably unrealistic for your ASD child due to his or her developmental disability, but also it is inconsistent with what is happening in society in general these days. Setting this expectation for your child is going to be hard not only because it is contrary to your ASD child's rate of development (the five-year delay can apply even into adulthood), but society has erected a number of other barriers to independence such as skyrocketing college tuition, a low minimum wage, the reduction of entry-level jobs, and increasing cost of living, to name a few. In many cases it makes sense to slow down and modify the post-18 plan.

Developmentally Ready

Does this mean that your child should play video games all day when they graduate from school? Your ASD child, like all children, needs to continue along the course of becoming a contributing member of society. Below is a list of skills and abilities I tell parents are essential in the course of becoming a fully functioning adult. The rate at which your child achieves these is going to be highly individualized, and you will likely need to exercise considerable patience in this process, but for those parents looking for a place to start, this is my list:

- Your child needs to be completely independent in going to bed and waking up at times that allow them to get enough sleep and be awake and productive when the rest of the world is awake and productive. Generally speaking, your child needs to be able to go to bed by 11pm and wake up by 7am, on his or her own, every single day.

- Your child needs to be able to manage his or her schedule with complete independence. This not only means keeping track of events (with the use of a calendar system), but also they need to be able to schedule things such as haircuts and doctor's appointments and keep them.

- Your child needs to be able to be completely independent in managing personal hygiene. This means your child takes showers and brushes his or her teeth, and does all the other hygiene activities (e.g., puts on deodorant) every day without reminders. Your child should always be wearing clean clothes. Your child should, without reminders, be washing clothing and bedding using a regular routine (e.g., weekly on Saturdays). They should never smell bad or look bad unless it is a time when people normally do (e.g., right after waking up, right after a workout).

- Your child needs to be completely independent in managing his or her belongings and his or her living space in a way that is consistent with the rules and expectations of the house. For instance, as long as your child is living in your home, your child needs to keep his or her room in a state of cleanliness that is consistent with your expectations, not their own. If your child chooses a strange outfit or style of dress that is outside what you find acceptable, they need to produce a picture or, better yet, a magazine that highlights their particular style.

- Your child needs to be completely independent when it comes to transportation. They need to either have their driver's license and be able to use it (have access to a car and be willing to drive), or be totally comfortable with public transportation, or have a reliable and fair way to share rides with people. Only under certain circumstances (e.g., physical disability, remote living situations) should getting around take anyone else's time but your child's (Mom should not be chauffeuring her 22-year-old son to his first day on the job).

- Your child needs to demonstrate the ability to give back to society, or contribute something without expecting a direct return. This could be something as simple as picking up trash in the neighborhood, volunteering at a soup kitchen, or other voluntary activity.

- Related to the point above, your child needs to have chores at home that do not necessarily involve cleaning up after himself or herself (which is a basic level expectation for younger ASD children anyway). This means that your child should be expected to clean a bathroom he or she does not use, clear other people's plates from the dinner table, or mow the lawn. The more your child shares in the running of the household the better, even it they do not do the activity as well as you can, or as quickly.

- Your child should have the ability or have a plan to manage his or her anxiety or other mental health problems, if applicable. This can (and probably should) include having his or her own therapist.

Start with these skills and see which ones your child can do consistently and thoroughly. Here is the progression of independent living skill mastery:

1. Are they able to do the task?

   a. Do they understand the skill?

   b. Do they have the mechanical and physical ability and means to do the task?

   c. Can they perform the task reliably (with the same outcome nine times out of the ten that they try)?

2. Can they do the activity with minimal reminders?

3. Can they do the activity with no reminders?

4. Is the activity incorporated into their daily lives (if they did not do it, could not do it, or forgot to do it, would they notice)?

Next, with your child (and any other member of the family who can participate—the more the better), begin to set goals. I would encourage you to focus on success—let success be the ultimate goal, and set goals that you all decide are ambitious but attainable. You can work on several of these at once, or pick and choose one at a time. Two weeks of consistently doing an activity is usually a good start to making the chore or activity a habit and part of the child's life (Step 4, above).

High Expectations

This list seems excessive to some parents, and rightly so. I see no problem with setting seemingly higher standards for ASD individuals who want to move out of the house than Neurotypical (NT) individuals. The reason is that NT individuals are generally more flexible and more likely than ASD individuals to self-advocate appropriately. Most NT individuals can pick things up as they go along. Most ASD individuals do not unless they are specifically taught to do so. The reason for this is two-fold. First, the "picking it up as you go along" strategy to learning requires a high level of Executive Functioning (EF) and organizational skills that most ASD individuals do not have. Second, most ASD individuals are going to be spending much of their time managing a lot of things that NT individuals are not even thinking about, or do not spend a lot of time thinking about, when they leave home. Sleeping in a new bed and in a new room, the massive change of routine, the brand new social structure and support structure—all of these things will likely be overwhelming to your ASD child and they will need to be able to depend on the skills they have mastered to get through the major upsets of transitions. Their lives will eventually return to routine, but they will have to find solace in the habits of waking up at a specific time, doing their laundry on their routine day, and filling out their daily schedule before they go to bed in the evening. Finally, there are supports out there for the person moving away from home for the first time, and especially at college, but your ASD child may not find them useful. For example, the "mixers" that colleges often put on for incoming students are social events designed to facilitate socializing. These events are generally mildly uncomfortable for most, but are likely going to be very off-putting for the average ASD individual.

The Alternative

The alternative to an independent adult is a dependent one. Some parents do choose to promote dependence in their adult children, and others just one day find themselves with a dependent adult child. You may believe that your child is unable to become independent. You may have tried in the past and met an unbelievable amount of resistance when you tried to instill some independence in them. You may shudder at the thought that your child would move out of the house and you would miss them terribly, or not be able to protect them adequately. There are more than a few households that, intentionally or unintentionally, allow their ASD child to stagnate or under-achieve in their independent living skills. These households should start thinking about who is going to take care of the child after the parents are unable to. Begin even now to talk to your ASD child's siblings, cousins, nieces, or nephews about ongoing care. Begin planning for their long-term financial needs. Consider looking at long-term care facilities for the future.

It is, of course, never too late. Regardless of your child's current level of independence, it can always improve. If you feel stuck, wait no longer and call a competent therapist.

Primary Factor

My boss, Kathryn Stewart, once told me that the number one factor in determining success for the ASD population is self-advocacy. There is a false belief that being independent means doing everything on our own and without help. The truth is that instances of such independence are actually quite rare in modern society. *Inter*dependence is actually a more reasonable goal. ASD individuals (and, really, all individuals) need to know how to ask for help when they really need it. This is a difficult skill for ASD individuals to learn. I think it is probably hard to decide when not-knowing something is legitimate (and I need to ask for help), and not-knowing something is part of the learning task (and I need to figure it out). Added to the mix, some ASD individuals have the experience of being treated as if they are mentally retarded (which they are not) or more helpless than they actually are, and have things done for them that they could do for themselves. I have known plenty of ASD students who will not think to ask for help understanding a question in an exam and simply sit and stare at it for the length of the test. On the other hand, I have known ASD students who seem to be unable to make any further progress in their work until they check in with their teacher to make sure what they have written is correct. Asking for help when you need it, versus figuring it out on your own, is truly a skill that requires a lot of practice, but it is one that I also believe is most predictive of success.

College and Vocation

There has been little to nothing traditional about your child up to this point, so why must they take the traditional path to college? By this I mean why do they need to complete their formal education by a certain age, immediately attend university for a set number of years to gain a degree, and then find an entry level job where they will rise in the ranks over the next 30 to 40 years? If this is your expectation for your child, I highly encourage you to reconsider and examine this expectation. Some parents might think that this is also what the child wants. Sometimes that buy-in and drive from your child is enough to actually make it happen, but there may be a time when you, the parent, need to reconsider the unrealistic dream and start working with your child to assemble a more realistic one.

How do you decide when it is time (to move out, go to college, get a job, become fully independent), and when your child might actually make it happen? Again, if there is an actual rush, or a need to achieve some sort of timeline or standard, then that will make the decision more simple. I have found that the vast majority of parents I have talked to who have such a timeline have adjusted it to better suit the developmental progress of their child after we discuss all options. What parents sometimes need is not another magical plan (there really is no secret here or magic to behold), it is getting the perspective of someone (like me) who has done this before, seen it play out, and can confirm that things are going to be okay.

I will encourage you to challenge what you believe about education and vocation. Is there really anything wrong with your child not following exactly in your path for education and employment? Will the less expensive college offer fewer opportunities than the more expensive one? How would your plans change if your child lived at home for another year, or couple of years? Is there any benefit in getting a job, joining the military, or working for a volunteer-based organization for a year, for example, before going to college? Would a trade school or skilled professional training be a good fit for your child? Think about your child's strengths and preferences when thinking about the future. It is my opinion that most ASD teens are smart enough to get into college, but not all would benefit from it. Consider consulting with an educational or vocational specialist about all the options. It can help to get a second opinion.

Practical Experience and the Possibility of Failure

There are a some experiences I recommend your child to have before finishing school that I think could have huge payoff, but there are a couple of things to consider. Your child needs to be placed in situations where there is a possibility of failure. To that end, your child needs to be allowed to make a mistake. Even if you can see it coming, and even if it looks semi-catastrophic (like it could get them fired), they need to be able to fail. The best time to make mistakes is when there are supports available to help you process and recover from the mistake, and get back on your feet stronger than before. You can be a part of that support system, but there should be at least one other adult who can provide adequate, practical support in the face of a major failure, such as a therapist, coach, clergy person, uncle, or other reasonable and compassionate adult that your ASD child has a relationship with and respects.

Here are some experiences your child should have before leaving school.

Job Interview

Job interviews are challenging for most people, but seem to be especially challenging for ASD teens and young adults. One interesting thing about a job interview: research says that they rarely offer any relevant information to the interviewer about how successful the person will be in the job. However, they are, unfortunately, almost essential for even the most menial jobs. Have your child attend job interviews, and ask for feedback from the interviewer about their performance. I have heard stories of teens putting their feet on the interviewer's desk, picking their nose, swearing, degrading and demeaning themselves (e.g., listing all of their faults) and the like. Job interview skill training and practice can be part of a child's Individual Education Plan (IEP). IEP goals can also be written to include support for completing résumés and job applications.

Internship

There is an internship program for ASD students at the school where I work and it has been one of the most meaningful and informative programs the school has designed. Each student has a high level of regular contact with a school-provided supervisor as well as a designated supervisor at the work-site. Work-site supervisors are trained how to give feedback to ASD students, and the focus is always on clarity and success. If you can find an adequate internship program for your child, I highly recommend you get them involved. I do not recommend you try to put one together yourself due to the level of skill and time it requires. Job coaches can be trained to work specifically with ASD individuals.

College Class

If you live near a community college or can otherwise enroll your child in one college class during the summer months (or when they are not inundated with their regular school work), it would be good for them to see what exactly are the expectations for a college class compared to a school class. They may notice that there is more work (and especially outside the classroom), the content is more sophisticated, there is higher expectation for class participation, and the students are generally smarter and more driven. Something my ASD clients who have taken a college class tell me is that they are surprised at how little their college professors care about their performance. This is the main difference, I have found, between school and college. School teachers are generally required to make sure you are successful (since education is generally mandatory). College, on the other hand, serves almost exclusively adults, and is voluntary.

Part-time Job

There is no legitimate downside to a part-time job. No experience required, low expectations, money in your pocket, flexible hours, and on and on. Most people you meet have great stories to tell about part-time jobs they had, and your child will be able to participate in those conversations with stories of his or her own.

Credit Card or Bank Card

Understanding the value and meaning of money can be tough for the ASD individual, and especially if they have never been denied anything they really want. Talk to your bank about options for teens for opening a bank account, and talk to them about programs for educating teens on how to manage money. I assure you they will overdraw their account (most of us have done this at one time), and there will be financial penalties, so be ready for that.

Travel

The other transformative (I do not use this word lightly) program I have been a part of for ASD teens has been an international travel program. I have no problems encouraging families to put off buying the new car, or get the second job, or the like to pay for the international trip for their ASD child, because I have seen how it can change children's lives by completely transforming their perspective on life. I have written an article published elsewhere on how to prepare and plan for the trip, how to pay for the trip, and how to process the trip with your child (Schlegelmilch 2010). The key is that your child is not traveling with you (the parent), but with another adult that can push them to do things on their own and generally have higher expectations for your child. These adults are also usually not embarrassed by your child's strange behavior. I have worked with many students over the years to set financial, independent living, and social goals in order to prepare for such trips.

The Changing Role of the Parent

It may not be clear from what I have written above, but I actually do advocate for an "over-involved" parenting style for very young ASD children. The world is not designed to meet the needs of your ASD child, and your child likely struggles with self-advocacy, so someone must step in to ensure needs are getting met. Parents need to be pit-bulls in IEP meetings, sit in on doctor's appointments, make themselves nuisances (if necessary) with school office staff, be in regular contact with teachers, talk with the soccer coach, and generally be okay with being referred to as a "helicopter parent," because that is usually what effective parenting of an ASD child looks like. The happiest parents seem to be those who understand the highly involved role they must play in the lives of their children, and are okay with being criticized by other parents who do not know how hard it is to raise a child with a developmental disability.

But you should not expect to play that role forever. You cannot call their college professors and advocate for them (in the US, for example, by law your child's professors cannot speak with you as your child is considered an adult on a college campus, regardless of their level of maturity). You cannot sit with them in job interviews, or go with them on dates when they are 40. There must be a time when you can back away and trust that your child can fulfill the necessary independent tasks for which you have trained them. Below is my understanding of the developmental stages of parenthood for parents of ASD individuals.

Infancy and Toddlerhood

A very early stage of parenting is one of discovery and experience. Parents have the job of enriching their child's life and learning, primarily through the senses. For some ASD children, toddlerhood is when they are identified to be on the Spectrum. Children may gain and then lose certain skills or positive habits (e.g., giving hugs) or fail to develop in certain ways (e.g., standing on one's own, speaking, gesturing). Parents are often cued in this stage that something is off, or their child needs some additional attention from a professional. Following these earliest diagnoses (Autism is currently diagnosed reliably as early as 24 months), parents scramble to put services in place. Early intervention is predictive of future positive outcomes, so time is of the essence. This might also be the time when parents realize their lives are going to be different than they expected. I can imagine priorities begin to shift and opinions form about what life will be like, or what it should be like.

Childhood

A group of Spectrum disorders (e.g., Asperger Syndrome [AS]) are diagnosed in childhood because the most obvious manifestations of the disability are social deficits. Children begin to socialize with an ever-increasing group of peers and adults when they start preschool and kindergarten (4–5 years old). Parents tell me that it is clear to them that their child has neither interest nor ability to interact and bond with their peers. Professionals might also think these ASD children have behavior problems as they struggle with the typical activities of childhood that stress doing what the group is doing, including sharing. What is probably happening is that the ASD child is trying desperately to regulate his or her sensory experience in a tumultuous environment (have you ever been in a preschool classroom?). Preschools and kindergartens specialize in bright and loud. Kids bump into each other, and it is still okay for teachers to hug and grab hands. ASD children often do not like this, and say so in brash ways that are often misread.

Parents sometimes report to me that they become their child's best friend during these years. They are their child's playmate because they understand best their child's nuanced sensory and social needs. They also (naturally) have a high level of empathy and patience for their child who does not necessarily like to play with others. Parents tell me they find that without their constant pushing, they are not confident their child would explore their environment at the level they need to in order to thrive. I think parents are making a tough but good decision at this time if they are being their child's best playmate. As if in contrast, ASD teens sometimes report to me that they have peers who have been their friends since early childhood. Their parents confirm that these children have known each other for a long time, but it is usually the case that the parents were friends and got together, and thus their children would be in proximity, but they would not necessarily "play." Parents also begin to experience the public school system at this time. They figure out quickly that their children are developmentally delayed, this delay will compound over time (peers will develop faster socially and in EF skills), and the school system is designed for the majority, not the minority. Many parents add "educational advocate" to the role of best friend with their child during these years.

Adolescence

Middle adolescence (15–16 years old) is when I have seen ASD teens start to understand the concept of peers and being a part of a group. This makes developmental sense because this process can happen around age 10 for NT children. Under the right circumstances (e.g., legitimate peer group, time spent together, adequate training and supervision for socializing) ASD children can start to develop friendships—real friendships. They do not have to settle for buddies (peers that are listening to parent instruction to "be nice" to the ASD child, see Chapter 3 for more on the differences between buddies and friends) and can start the process of getting their social and emotional needs met by peers.

This process can be extremely long and arduous, and most parents of ASD teens tell me they manage 99 percent of their child's emotional and social needs. Parents also mention that they can begin to see a day when their ASD child will not be completely dependent on them socially and emotionally. This makes some parents sad, some hopeful, and most have a mixture of both feelings. Adolescence is the beginning of the backing-off stage for most parents who have ASD children whose behavior is under control, are performing fairly well in school, are getting their organizational and EF needs addressed (by the school or other professional), and have a group of peers that have the potential to become friends.

Some parents are not thinking about independence, and cannot imagine considering it because the school is not doing what it needs to do, or their child has a complex mental health or physical health issue, or is still the target of bullying, or any number of events or circumstances out of the parents' control that have become the focus of attention. Some parents are desperately waiting for their child to graduate and be done with school so they can get a break from the school's expectations. I tell parents all the time that school life has very little to do with adult life, and if, after leaving school, your child no longer wants to wake up very early, sit in various classrooms for seven hours a day, and do work he or she finds uselessly repetitive and boring, it is not hard to create a different life. Adulthood is, in many respects, much more flexible than adolescence and school life.

Post-school

The older one gets, the fewer and less concrete the expectations for development. In adulthood, what was once considered "weird" becomes "quirky." Twenty-year-olds in school look strange, but 30-year-olds in college are common. The parent/child relationship in the post-school years seems to be a relief for some parents. After all, there is less of a constant daily reminder that your children are different from other children. On the other hand, parents tell me that since there are fewer standards, deciding on the correct path for parenting and expectations can be more of a challenge.

From what I can tell, social, emotional, and EF development continues into adulthood for most ASD individuals who set and work toward goals in these areas. The difference is that there is less of a daily reminder about the developmental disability or delay since their children are not necessarily going to school with same-age peers, and the window of "typical" behavior in adulthood seems to expand. I encourage parents in these years to continue to expect higher levels of independence and productivity from their adult children. Parents often tell me that they want to treat their children like adults, and really want that relationship to become more egalitarian. Some parents tell me they worry that without constant encouragement and pushing, their child would stop moving forward socially, emotionally, and vocationally.

In my experience, young adulthood is when ASD individuals can more effectively look at their peers and get a realistic sense of where their lives are relative to their same-age peers. In some cases the assessment is very positive, in others it can be depressing. Parents do well, post-school, to continue to direct their ASD children to their same-age peers for things such as emotional and social support, employment aspirations, and independent living skills. Half-steps to independence include things such as getting an apartment with another same-age ASD peer, and the parents of each peer taking turns doing weekly spot-checks on the apartment. Completing college can look like taking two classes at first, and then adding a third class later until you find the critical mass for hours spent in the classroom each day. The point is that each decision needs to be moving toward a greater level of responsibility and independence.

And Beyond

In my experience, ASD individuals and their parents have a tighter, more symbiotic and reciprocal bond than most parents and their children. There is a common understanding between this individual with developmental disabilities who has fought for all their accomplishments and his or her parents who have, for better or worse, devoted their life and formed their identity around raising the happiest, most successful child they can raise. I admire the bond I see between most ASD individuals and their parents. Although not always polite and productive, the bond is deep and stable. The bond between ASD individuals and their parents often sets the standard for parent/child relationships in my book. Please do not deny this bond, or feel ashamed about it, or take it for granted. We are all human, after all, and we need each other. Bonds like these defy disability and redefine normal.

REFERENCES

Alloy, L.B., and Abramson, L.Y. (1979) "Judgment of contingency in depressed and nondepressed students: sadder but wiser?" *Journal of Experimental Psychology: General 108*, 441–485.

American Psychiatric Association (1994) *Diagnostic and Statistical Manual of Mental Disorders, 4th Edition.* Washington, DC: American Psychiatric Association.

American Psychiatric Association (2013) *Diagnostic and Statistical Manual of Mental Disorders, 5th Edition.* Washington, DC: American Psychiatric Association.

Asperger, H. [1944]; translated and annotated by Frith, U. (1991) " 'Autistic Psychopathy' in Childhood." In U. Frith (ed.) *Autism and Asperger Syndrome.* Cambridge: Cambridge University Press.

Attwood, T. (1998) *Asperger's Syndrome: A Guide for Parents and Professionals.* London: Jessica Kingsley Publishers.

Baumrind, D. (1966) "Effects of authoritative parental control on child behavior." *Child Development 37*, 4, 887–907.

Happé, F., and Frith, U. (2006) "The weak coherence account: detail-focused cognitive style in autism spectrum disorders." *Journal of Autism and Developmental Disorders 36*, 1, 5–25.

Kohlberg, L. (1981) *Essays on Moral Development, Vol. I: The Philosophy of Moral Development.* San Francisco, CA: Harper & Row.

Mischel, W., Ebbesen, E.B., and Raskoff Zeiss, A. (1972) "Cognitive and attentional mechanisms in delay of gratification." *Journal of Personality and Social Psychology 21*, 2, 204–218.

Rourke, B.P. (1995) *Syndrome of Nonverbal Learning Disabilities: Neurodevelopmental Manifestations.* New York, NY: Guilford Press.

Schlegelmilch, A. (2010) "Traveling with children on the autism spectrum." *Special Education Advisor.* Available at www.specialeducationadvisor.com/traveling-with-children-on-the-autism-spectrum, accessed on 4 October 2013.

Seligman, M.E.P. (1972) "Learned helplessness." *Annual Review of Medicine 23*, 1, 407–412.

Seligman, M.E.P., and Maier, S.F. (1967) "Failure to escape traumatic shock." *Journal of Experimental Psychology 74*, 1–9.

Soraya, L. (2013a) "New research on autism and suicide." *Psychology Today*, 3/13/13. Available at www.psychologytoday.com/blog/aspergers-diary/201303/new-research-autism-and-suicide, accessed on 4 October 2013.

Soraya, L. (2013b) *Living Independently on the Autism Spectrum*. London: Adams Media Corporation.

Stanford, A. (2011) *Business for Aspies: 42 Best Practices for Using Asperger Syndrome Traits at Work Successfully*. London: Jessica Kingsley Publishers.

Stewart, K. (2007) *Helping a Child with Nonverbal Learning Disorder or Asperger's Disorder* (2nd edition). Oakland, CA: New Harbinger Press.

INDEX

Made in the USA
Las Vegas, NV
19 June 2021